'*Ye Olde Townships*'

DENBY DALE, SKELMANTHORPE, CLAYTON WEST & DISTRICT

By the same author:

Denebi – Farmstead of the Danes
(Richard Netherwood, 1997)

A History of the Denby Dale Pies
(J R Nicholls, 1998)

Denby & District – From Prehistory to the Present
(Wharncliffe Books, 2001)

Denby & District II – From Landed Lords to Inspired Industrialists
(Wharncliffe Books, 2004)

Denby & District III – From Medieval Manuscripts to Modern Memories
(Wharncliffe Books, 2006)

'Ye Olde Townships' – Denby Dale, Scissett, Ingbirchworth and District
(Wharncliffe Books, 2007)

'Ye Olde Townships' – Skelmanthorpe, Clayton West and District
(Wharncliffe Books, 2007)

Denby & District IV – Chronicles of Clerics, Convicts, Corn Millers & Comedians
(Wharncliffe Books, 2009)

The Denby Dale Pies – Ten Giants 1788–2000
(Wharncliffe Books, 2012)

'Ye Olde Townships'

DENBY DALE, SKELMANTHORPE, CLAYTON WEST & DISTRICT

A Further Selection

A Denby & District Archive Photograph Album

CHRIS HEATH

with
Susan Buckley and Stanley Sheead

Wharncliffe Books

First published in Great Britain in 2014 by
Wharncliffe Books
an imprint of
Pen & Sword Books Ltd
47 Church Street
Barnsley
South Yorkshire
S70 2AS

ISBN 978 1 47382 365 5

A CIP catalogue record for this book is
available from the British Library

Typeset in Palatino by Chic Graphics

Printed and bound in England
by CPI Group (UK) Ltd, Croydon, CR0 4YY

Pen & Sword Books Ltd incorporates the imprints of
Pen & Sword Aviation, Pen & Sword Family History, Pen & Sword Maritime,
Pen & Sword Military, Pen & Sword Discovery, Wharncliffe Local History,
Wharncliffe True Crime, Wharncliffe Transport, Pen & Sword Select,
Pen & Sword Military Classics, Leo Cooper, Remember When,
The Praetorian Press, Seaforth Publishing and Frontline Publishing

For a complete list of Pen & Sword titles please contact
PEN & SWORD BOOKS LIMITED
47 Church Street, Barnsley, South Yorkshire, S70 2AS, England
E-mail: enquiries@pen-and-sword.co.uk
Website: www.pen-and-sword.co.uk

Contents

Dedication

For Paul, Dave, Rupes and Seren –

Here's to DHIII

Acknowledgements

With thanks to my co-contributors – Susan Buckley and Stanley Sheead, without whom this book would not have come about and with whom it has, as always, been a pleasure to work.

Further grateful thanks must go to:
Charles Hewitt, Jonathan Wilkinson, Sylvia Menzies-Earl, Dean Wyatt, Keeley, Abby & Libby Whittaker, Kate Gill-Martin, Phillip Brook and my Mum, Dad and Brother for their help and support. Finally I must apologise to my dog, Seren, who has lain on the bed snoring with boredom whilst I wrote this. There will be plenty of time for walks now!

Any errors or omissions are entirely the fault of the author. Whilst every effort has been made to trace the copyright owners of the illustrations in this book the author wishes to apologise to anyone who has not been acknowledged. If an error has occurred this will be corrected in any subsequent reprint of this work.

Introduction

The Upper Dearne Valley, incorporating the larger villages of Clayton West, Denby Dale and Skelmanthorpe has a rich and fascinating history. It has been my privilege to have been able to uncover much that was previously lost and weave together the many strands that tell the tale of the area and its people. My first book was published in 1997 and promptly sold out within a few months encouraging further efforts and renewed determination to discover and publish as much as possible to educate, inform and above all, entertain the reader. No village lives in isolation and so I found myself learning about areas that initially I had no intention of researching. Every village has its own local historian, history society or knowledgeable enthusiast but for many years this knowledge was held privately only to be made public by way of lectures illustrated by slides displaying images of fascinating but all too brief local scenes from many years ago. Thankfully, that situation has long since changed. As I have looked into the different villages in the Upper Dearne I have met some wonderful people, who have shared my desire to see information and photographs shared with the people who live in the hills and dales of the valley, by having them published.

This book contains hundreds of images never published before, though with the benefit of experience, many more will come to light in the years after this publication. No matter how diligently one searches, there will always be the one that got away, though I believe it will be many years before enough can be assembled to produce another photographic book such as this. This book is the third in the 'Ye Olde Townships' series, originally planned to complement the 'Denby & District' series they have proved so popular that the 'Clayton West, Skelmanthorpe & District' volume has been out of print for some time now. I have always endeavoured to illustrate my words with as many pictures as possible. History was not dry and boring when it was happening, so it is important to try and keep it as fresh as possible when recording and relating it. One photograph is worth a page of words and this book is full of them.

Family and local history has now become an incredibly popular pastime, even spawning television shows in prime time slots and huge fairs held at National exhibition centres. The United Kingdom is embracing its past in a way that has never happened before. The advent of the internet facilitates much of this in a way that I could never have imagined when I set out on my voyage of discovery. I initially learned to research using the old methods and have now embraced the modern opportunities but one thing always guaranteed to bring a new

The author with his Border Collie, Seren, taken at the George Inn, Upper Denby.

sense of wonder is the first sight of an old photograph, never before seen. At forty-four years old there is still time for me to see even more change as an infinite number of records and information go online every year. Perhaps it is time I went back to researching my own family history, which has been languishing, stuck, in 1720 for well over twenty years.

I have included one or two photographs in this collection that have appeared in previous works. The reason for this is largely because I didn't feel that they had been produced at the right size or quality and that justice had not been done to them. I hope my readers will forgive this very minor duplication. I have also included a section at the end of some of the chapters entitled 'Selected Notes'. These include details and photographs that would once have been used as part of a Denby & District book. That series is now at an end, but it would be remiss of me not to update previous stories or threads where new information has come to light or to ignore my own recent research, such as the details concerning the family of Thomas Fitzgerald Wintour, Rector of High Hoyland.

When I began to research and write, very little local history was commercially available for Denby Dale, Skelmanthorpe, Clayton West and all the other villages within the Upper Dearne Valley. When interviewed by the local press or radio channels the usual question came up time and again – why did I write it? My stock answer was the truth – because of the very dearth of material and the reliance on antiquarian publications and that the area was largely ignored in most modern publications. Little by little, thanks to the support of my publisher and most of all my readers the balance has changed. One book reviewer from 2009 suggested that:

> *Denby Dale's history must now be one of the best-documented of all British villages.*

I doubt he was correct and the comment, I believe, was tongue in cheek, but I'm quite happy with it.

Chris Heath
April 2014

The Townships

Clayton West

A village promotional postcard dating from 1905.

Spring Grove from Cliffe End, Beanland's Mill can be seen to the centre right.

The old pack horse bridge at Park Mill.

The Junction Inn at Park Mill on Wakefield Road around 1900.

The Junction Inn at Park Mill on Wakefield Road showing the colliery railway gantry overhead prior to the First World War.

Houses on Wakefield Road at Park Mill.

Back Road, Park Mill. The building in the centre was a motor spares and bike shop; the sign on the wall is for Raleigh bicycles.

A view through trees of houses towards the bottom of Scott Hill.

Park View on Scott Hill leading down towards Park Mill, circa 1900.

A view of High Street in 1911.

High Street taken around the turn of the nineteenth century. The Commercial Inn is on the left.

Scott Hill looking up towards High Street, Park Lodge is to the left. The building with the high pitched roof in the centre of the photograph was the church school, which, amongst other things hosted pantomimes and concerts. It has now been demolished.

The entrance to Church Lane, All Saints Church is in the centre.

Church Lane, leading off from Guide Post Corner.

Guide Post Corner, the Police House can be seen to the left with the badge above the door. The Post Office is the building furthest to the right.

Guide Post, the Duke William Inn is on the right.

High Street, Church Lane turns off to the left by the Duke William Inn, circa 1900.

High Street, the Duke William Inn is to the right, the Guide Post has by now been removed.

Frank Stafford's butchers shop on High Street in 1905.

Hill Top Road, Clayton West, circa 1900.

Hill Top Road, taken
in February 1977.

Hill Top Road,
Clayton West.

Hill Top Road, circa 1900.

A horse and carriage begins the ascent of Bank End heading towards High Hoyland. Hill Top Farm can be seen in the centre of this early twentieth century photograph.

A horse and carriage descend from Bank End heading down to the top of Clayton West.

Houses at Holmfield with Kaye's Council School and schoolhouse in the background. The single storey building in the foreground to the right was Ernest Bedford's joinery shop.

The Shoulder of Mutton, Church Lane, dating to the period between the World Wars.

Chapel Hill, showing the United Reform Church. This chapel opened in 1866 as a Congregational Chapel at a cost of £1000. In 1973 following the union of the Presbyterian and Congregational churches it became the United Reform Church.

Square Fold, circa. 1900.

Chapel Hill, 1907. Mount Tabor Wesleyan Reform Chapel (opened June 1867) dominates the photograph.

Chapel Hill, early twentieth century.

Spring Grove, at the bottom of Chapel Hill heading towards Scissett. The National school can be seen in the distance to the centre left.

Station Road at the bottom of Scott Hill taken from the railway lines. Alec Buckley of Vinery Farm, Clayton West, once farmed the field across from the houses.

Station Rd. Clayton West.

Holmfield Road, looking down towards the Congregational Chapel, later the United Reform Church.

Willie Sheard, Clayton West Town Clerk, outside his home on Bilham Road.

Bilham Road, early twentieth century.

Newlands Avenue, off Church Lane and just to the West of Holmfield Road.

Park Lodge, off Scott Hill.

Interior of All Saint's Church.

School & House
Clayton West.

Kaye's Council school and schoolhouse, off Holmfield Road, early twentieth century.

A slightly different view of Kaye's Council school and the schoolhouse.

The Rectory, Clayton West. Horace Gordon Lowe had replaced the Rev. Thomas Fitzgerald Wintour at High Hoyland having arrived in 1898. After his marriage to the daughter of John Edward Kaye, estate agent to Bretton Hall the couple went to live at Woodlands in Scissett as the Rectory at High Hoyland was still in the occupation of the former Rector's wife who had taken the option to purchase the property. A rectory in Clayton West was a much more suitable option and when some land was made available, at the end of Bilham Road, by the Bretton Estate it was considered suitable for a parsonage house.

The Rectory, Clayton West, built in the late Victorian period at a cost of £2000. The money was raised by a mortgage through Queen Anne's Bounty and the debt paid off within four years. This photograph was probably taken soon after building work was completed.

The late Victorian Rectory. The building had an enormous garden, servants' quarters and a butler's pantry. The Rev. Lowe left the incumbency of High Hoyland and Clayton West in 1902.

Dearnlea, Clayton West.

Cliffe House, Clayton West.

The Cliffe
Clayton West.

Park House, once home to local textile manufacturer John Kaye who was a highly influential figure in the development of Clayton West, the village school still bears his name.

Park House, off Bilham Road, Clayton West.

Ridingwood Lodge, Clayton West.

Ridingwood Lodge and grounds, Clayton West.

Holmfield, Clayton West.

Ashville, 31 Church Lane, Clayton West. Formerly home to Arthur Mellor Beardsell, once a partner at Beanland's textile manufacturing business, the brother in law of William Thompson Beanland.

Cottages on Common Lane, to the left hand side before heading towards Swallow Hills and Deffer Wood.

Clayton West Railway, junction cabin, early twentieth century. The line opened in 1879 but was closed to goods traffic in 1970. By this time it had been downgraded to a public delivery siding. Final closure of the line took place in 1983.

Clayton West Station, a general view of the platform dated June 1963.

Clayton West Station and platform, 1969.

Clayton West station cabin in 1969.

A further view of the station cabin in 1969.

The 1:00pm train to Huddersfield as it leaves Clayton West Station on 5 September 1980, approaching the signal box before travelling on to the single line.

Railway wreckage at Clayton West after coal trucks had broken loose at Skelmanthorpe in 1913.

A view of Clayton West Station from the buffer stops, a three-car class 110 DMU arrives from Huddersfield on 5 September 1980.

Trackside crane, near Clayton West.

Clayton West Colliery, early twentieth century.

Clayton West football team, Huddersfield Red Triangle Under 18 Section Champions 1950-51. Back row, left to right: A Firth, J A Rawley (Chairman), G Fisher, D Brook, B Glover, B Guest, N Gaunt, W Hawke, B Bedford, J B Fisher. Front row, left to right: E Booth (Secretary), G Guest, A Jackson, K Armitage, A Firth (Captain), J Taylor, E Hepworth, L Taylor (trainer), H Senior.

An old chimney undergoing controlled demolition on Bilham Road. The former premises of the *Huddersfield & District Chronicle* newspaper can be seen to the right.

Clayton West football team, taken outside the Woodman during the 1957-58 season when they won the Barlow Cup.

Clayton West Brass Band in 1936.

Cliffe Gardens, Clayton West. The former mill owner, Hardy Beanland (1874-1934), originally laid out Cliffe Woods Park, in an area of old quarries, which had originally supplied stone for local road building. In the wood there are small stone boundary markers with the letters BHA on them. It is believed that they mark the boundary between common land and that owned by Beanland's mill.

Brady Webster & Son, grocers and provision merchants, on the right hand side of High Street, heading up through Clayton West.

Cliffe Gardens.

Waterfall at Cliffe Park. Cliffe Woods are today owned by Kirklees Council and are managed as a community woodlands project by Cliffe Woods Conservation Group.

Selected Historical Notes

Bilham Grange, built by the Allott family during the seventeenth century, probably replacing an earlier structure.

Bilham Grange and the Allott family

The earliest members of the Allott family in the area were Adam, Thomas and John who were tenants on land at Emley owned by Byland Abbey during the reign of King Henry III (1216-1272). The family residence was at Bentley Grange, which came into possession of King Henry VIII after his suppression of the monasteries during the reformation. Byland Abbey was dissolved in 1538 and in 1543 Elizabeth Allott (the widow of Robert Allott who died in 1541) bought the Bentley Grange and its dependent lands. This lady, who was a sister of Armigael Waad the navigator and niece to Comyn, the Prior of Nostell was highly influential in the advancement of the family. Elizabeth also bought lands at Crigglestone on which a younger son was settled. Lands in Holmfirth were secured by marriage in the next generation by a marriage with a member of the Charlesworth family. Further marriages with the Wentworth family of Bretton and the Saviles of Thornhill brought the Allotts into connection with two of the most powerful families in the West Riding. This was further strengthened by the marriage of Richard Allott of Bilham Grange with Grace Wentworth, the sister of Sir Thomas and Sir Mathew Wentworth.

The first Allott to dwell at Bilham Grange and possibly the man responsible for the present building was Bartin Allott who was born in 1581. As the Allotts of Bentley Grange continued with the family of Bartin's elder brother, John, Bartin established his dynasty at Bilham Grange. He was described as of Bentley Grange, then Thorpe in Almondbury and then of Bilham Grange where he appears to have died in 1648 which dates the house to the first half of the seventeenth century. Bartin's son, Richard (1617-1674) attended Wakefield school in 1633 and is the Richard referred to above who married Grace Wentworth. They lived at Bilham Grange and had at least three children. The eldest of these and heir was another Bartin Allott born in 1656. He became a Lieutenant in the Militia in 1689 and married Mary, the daughter and co-heir of John Peebles of Dewsbury. Bartin was the last member of the family to hold that name and his death in 1701 meant that his son, Brian, now inherited Bilham Grange.

Brian Allott was destined for a life in the church. Born in 1693, he matriculated in 1712 aged 19 and later held the livings of Stinton, Nottinghamshire in 1734, Londesborough, Yorkshire in 1736 and finally, Kirkheaton in 1757 until his death in 1773. This last appointment allowed him to dwell at Bilham Grange and bring up his family with his wife, Margaret, the daughter and co-heir of Nicholas Wilmot of Osmaston. Brian's sister, Grace married Joseph Oates of Nether Denby in 1706 and produced sixteen children (see Denby & District V1 for further details of the Oates family). When Brian died the antiquarian historian, Joseph Hunter described him as:

much beloved by his friends among whom was Garrick who wrote these lines to be inscribed upon his tomb –

> *More with love than with the fear of God*
> *This vale of sorrows he cheerfully trod.*
> *So tuned to harmony, and hating strife,*
> *From youth to age unclouded was his life,*
> *Nought could his earthly virtuous joys increase,*
> *But heavenly song and everlasting peace.*

Brian and Margaret had at least five children, the eldest of whom was another Brian. This second Brian had originally followed a military career but he finally followed in his father's footsteps and took Holy orders, eventually becoming the Rector of Burnham in Norfolk. He was also rather profligate and in 1779, only six years after his father's death his financial affairs were in disarray. His living had been sequestered and he found himself in prison. To solve his crisis Bilham Grange was put up for sale and it was expected that Sir Thomas Blackett would purchase it. This did eventually happen but not until 1790 when Thomas gave £6105 for it. Rev. Brian Allott did weather the storm however, which we know from the existence of a congratulatory letter he sent to the Rector of his old living at Burnham. The letter was sent to Rev. Edmund Nelson (1722-1802) and regarded the successful activities of his son at the Battle of the Nile in 1798, his son, being, of course, the then, Rear Admiral Horatio Nelson.

Allot Family of Bentley Grange and Bilham Grange

Thomas Allott

John Allott

Robert Allott — -1541 — Residence: Bentley Grange

Elizabeth Waad — -1566

Robert Allott — 1530 - 1605 — Residence: Bentley Grange

Jannet Charlesworth — -1610

John Allott

Elizabeth Allott

Alyson Allott

Margaret Allott

John Allott — Residence: Bentley Grange

Jennet Mitchel

Brice Allott — 1563 - 1639

Mathew Allott

Edward Allott

BENTLEY GRANGE LINE

Bartin Allott — 1581 - 1648 — Residence: Bilham Grange

Grace Bims — -1643 — Married: 1610 in Almondbury

Dorothy Allott

Elizabeth Allott

Margaret Allott

Ethelred Allott

Richard Allott — 1617 - 1674 — Residence: Bilham Grange

Grace Wentworth — -1681 — Married: 1640 in Darton

Ann Allott

Grace Allott

Dorothy Allott

Bartin Allott — 1656 - 1701 — Residence: Bilham Grange

Mary Peebles — -1696 — Married: 1682

Wentworth Allott

Elizabeth Allott

Catherine Allott

Mary Allott — 1677 -

Sarah Allott — 1679 -

Elizabeth Allott — 1682 -

Anne Allott — 1684 -

Grace Allott — 1685 - 1748

Joseph Oates

OATES @ NETHER DENBY

George Allott — 1686 -

Jane Allott — 1689 -

Brian Allott — 1693 - 1773 — Residence: Bilham Grange

Margaret Wilmot

Brian Allott — Residence: Bilham Grange

Mary Kennedy — Married: 1761

Valentine Henry Allott

Richard Allott

Anna Margaretta Allott

Mary Allott

Brian Montgomery Allott — 1762 - Infant

Catherine M. Allott — 1763 - 1812

Spring Grove House built by William Norton in 1826.

Spring Grove House and the Beanland family

William was the eldest son of Benjamin Norton and older brother to the future Scissett textile manufacturing magnates, Joseph (Nortonthorpe Hall) and George (Bagden Hall). William built Spring Grove Mills and began manufacturing textiles from 1825 but the depression in 'fancy weaving' in 1826 saw the business and premises pass to a partnership between John Wood (a worsted manufacturer from Bradford) and Charles Walker (spinners of Bradford). The new business ran under the name of Messrs. Wood and Walker. Charles Walker and his family lived at Spring Grove House. In 1869 Charles Walker sold the business to R Beanland & Co. worsted spinners and top makers of Bradford for £8500.

Robert Beanland, known as 'Old Bob', was born in 1805 and married Hannah Thompson who was nine years his junior. Their eldest son was christened William Thompson Beanland, perpetuating Hannah's family name. Robert and William, along with Isaac Naylor (who had married William's sister Jemima) took up their new business in December 1869. By 1879 the partnership with Isaac Naylor was severed after serious financial losses. When Robert Beanland died, in 1890, the business passed on to his son, William Thompson Beanland (who lived at Spring Grove House until his death in 1914). In 1892 William took on a partnership with Arthur Mellor Beardsell (who had married William Beanland's daughter, Hannah Matilda) and George Baker Hey. We can find William in the 1871 census returns at Spring Grove House:

Name	Age	Yr. Born	Birthplace
William Thompson Beanland	32	1838	Yorkshire
Mary Ann Beanland	30	1796	Yorkshire
Lillian Beanland	2	1869	Devon
Thompson B Beanland	1	1870	Yorkshire
Hannah Matilda Beanland	0	1871	Yorkshire
Ann Hopper	25	1846	Yorkshire
Abigail Hinchliffe	21	1850	Yorkshire

The Beanland Family

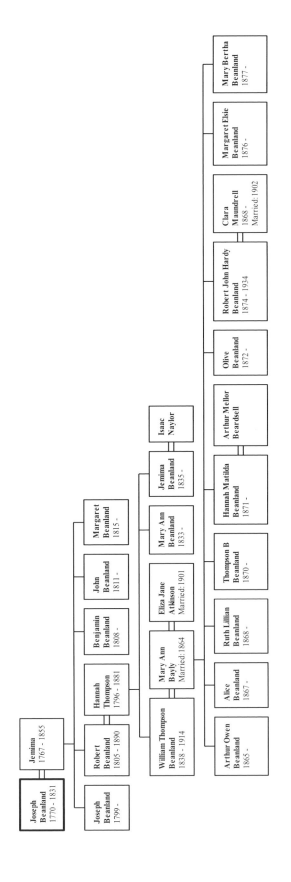

Joseph Beanland 1770 - 1831

Jemima 1767 - 1855

Joseph Beanland 1799 -

Robert Beanland 1805 - 1890

Hannah Thompson 1796 - 1881

Benjamin Beanland 1808 -

John Beanland 1811 -

Margaret Beanland 1815 -

William Thompson Beanland 1838 - 1914

Mary Ann Bayly Married: 1864

Eliza Jane Atkinson Married: 1901

Mary Ann Beanland 1833 -

Jemima Beanland 1835 -

Isaac Naylor

Arthur Owen Beanland 1865 -

Alice Beanland 1867 -

Ruth Lillian Beanland 1868 -

Thompson B Beanland 1870 -

Hannah Matilda Beanland 1871 -

Arthur Mellor Beardsell

Olive Beanland 1872 -

Robert John Hardy Beanland 1874 - 1934

Clara Maundrell 1868 - Married: 1902

Margaret Elsie Beanland 1876 -

Mary Bertha Beanland 1877 -

William Thompson Beanland and Mary Ann Bayly were married in 1864 though sometime after 1877 Mary Ann passed away. William did re-marry, but not until 1901, to Eliza Jane Atkinson.

William Thompson Beanland's son, Robert John Hardy Beanland (know as Hardy) joined the partnership in 1896 aged 22. Hardy lived at the Old Hall at Emley and became the last member of the Beanland family name to hold a partnership within the company, though future Directors were related via marriages to the founders. On 22 December 1924 Hardy left England from the port of Bristol bound for Kingston, Jamaica, he sailed aboard the Camito which was to take him as far as Cristobal, Panama where he would obtain another ship. December departures abroad seem to have been the norm for Hardy as we know that he also visited Quebec in Canada and on 15 December 1932 left London on board the Cathay bound for Brisbane, Australia, his ultimate destination was Colombo, Ceylon (now Sri Lanka). Whether these were business trips or simply a case of wanderlust to see exotic new locations is currently unknown. When Hardy died in 1934 members of the Beardsell and Dew families carried on operations at Spring Grove Mill. Even today amongst locals, the remaining mill buildings are still known as Beanland's, which when one considers that the mill closed down in 1975 is testament indeed to the influence this family once had on the area.

The mill premises of Robert Beanland & Co. Ltd., Spring Grove Mills, Clayton West, circa 1900.

Cumberworth

Above and Below: Salem Wesleyan Reform Union Church.
Established in 1871, the congregation originally used a room at a property on Barnsley Road for meetings. The chapel was built on Barnsley Road in 1879 and closed in 1990. This church never became part of the United Methodist Free Churches.

Founded by William and Smith Wilkinson, the chapel is now a private residence. Smith Wilkinson & Sons were recorded as woollen drapers in Cumberworth in 1912, though by 1936 they were listed as tailors.

Upper Cumberworth C of E school. Built in 1820 as a National School and enlarged in 1894. By 1912 it was described as a Public Elementary School when Henry Johnson was the Master. By 1922 Miss Beatrice Senior had taken over as Mistress. Photo dated 1904.

Scholars pose for a photograph outside Cumberworth school in 1906.

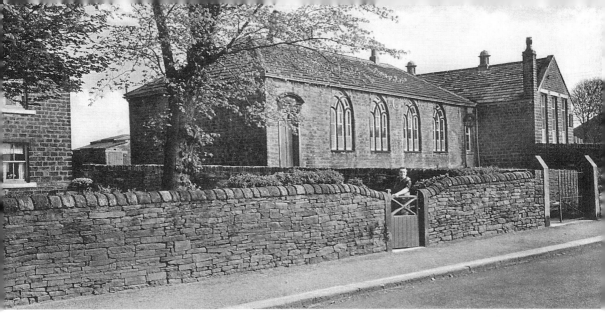

The Grade II listed school building on Cumberworth Lane, showing the gothic arches. The 1901 trade directory records that the average attendance was 98 pupils and that the Master was Edward Hoyland.

Crowds witness the stone laying ceremony for the erection of the Sunday school for the Primitive Methodist Chapel at Lower Cumberworth. Both Upper and Lower Cumberworth were preaching centres in the Barnsley Primitive Methodist Circuit during the 1820's when private houses were used for services. The chapel was built in 1851 at a cost of £210 with a seating capacity of 160 and an annual attendance of 100. The Chapel was enlarged in 1877. The Sunday school was built next door in 1908. A large room under the Sunday school was used as a village institute until the 1960's, it was renovated in 1972 - 1973 for use as a community room.

School Feast at Cumberworth in 1909.

A further scene of the School Feast at Cumberworth in 1909.

Upper Cumberworth C of E School Class one pupils in 1918.
Back, left to right – Moorhouse Beaumont, Herbert Shaw, Fred Heywood, ? Smith, George Robinson, Sam Peace, Dudley Peach.
Middle row, left to right – Reuben Smith, Bertram Peace, Gordon Turton, Gertrude Peace, Daisy Nichols, Winifred Jackman, Doris Brooke, Ivo Smith, George Horner, Frank Heeley.
Seated, left to right – Harriet Peace, Gwendoline Firth, Lillian Peace, Rose Nichols, Eliza Peace, Katy Smith, Lucy Taylor, Eric Jackman.
The teacher at the extreme back right is Miss Beatrice Kilner.

Upper Cumberworth C of E pupils, 1952/3.
Back row – D Stephenson, D Barraclough, M Wainwright, P Rawson, D Hudson.
Front row – I Wainwright, E Womersley, A Appleyard, M Leeming, A Sharp, M Charlesworth.

Upper Cumberworth C of E pupils, 1952/3.
Back row, left to right: David Wainwright, Keith Smith, Tony Schofield, Peter Roebuck, Steven Hirst.
Middle row, left to right: Michael Brown, Roger Swain, Barbara Hardy, Celia Beaumont, Joan Stephenson, Patricia Hudson, Derek Womersley, Robert Brisby.
Front row, left to right: Joan Clay, Delia Smith, Sandra Oades, Linda Hirst, Sandra Faxon, Glenys Turton, Joyce Womersley.

An advertising postcard for William Barraclough & Son, Motor Dealers of Upper Cumberworth. The model shown was available from the 1920's until just after the end of World War Two. William Barraclough was recorded as a farmer in 1912. By 1922 he had opened a post office in Cumberworth and in 1936 (now joined by his son), he was recorded as a haulage contractor. It was only a short step to begin selling cars. The post office had by this time been augmented with a grocers shop and was run by William's relative, Joseph Barraclough. The phone number for all these activities was constant, High Flatts 12.

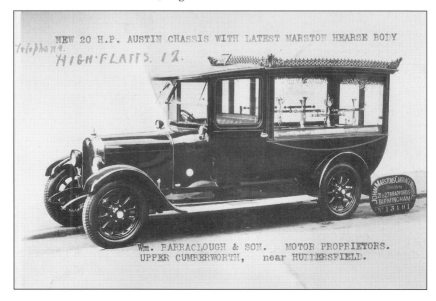

The ladies of Lower Cumberworth Methodist Church in the 1960's.
From back left – G Lockwood, K Lockwood, A Pell, A E Firth, E Rollinson, J Lockwood, E Lockwood, M Lockwood, E Tarbett, ? Turton, A M Rhodes, G Littlewood, C Lockwood.

Cumberworth football squad 1921/2, known affectionately as the Nibs.
Back row, left to right: Harold Auckland, Frank Kilner, Fenton Shaw, Fenton Senior, Clarence H Prince, Willie Senior.
Front row, left to right: Maurice Senior, Clifford Prince, Frank Auckland, Joe Hoyle, Harry Horn.

Denby Dale

WAKEFIELD ROAD

THE VIADUCT

HOLY TRINITY CHURCH

DENBY DALE

HIGHWOOD LODGE, KITCHENROYD

DD.15

MEMORIAL GARDENS

A promotional postcard dating from the mid-twentieth century.

An overview of the village. The roof of Kenyon's mills can be seen in the centre. John Brownhill's factory can be seen to the right. Circa 1920's.

The mills of Jonas Kenyon and the Corn Mill are to the centre of the photograph. From the left towards the centre, houses on Sunny Bank can be seen. To the right Miller Hill snakes its way out of the village.

Taken from the top of the viaduct, Bank Lane continues the last part of its run from Upper Denby past the terraced cottages at the side of the River Dearne. The old tin church can be seen in the bottom right of the photograph.

Catch Bar corner, from a postcard dated 1943.

Rockwood Lodge, left of Catch Bar Corner, looking down Wakefield Road towards Denby Dale. Circa 1940.

A view looking back to Catch Bar Corner and Rockwood Lodge, circa mid 1950's.

CARR BRIDGE DENBY DALE

Carr Bridge, the footpath heading right on the picture heads up towards Toby Wood. The bridge was a favourite spot for photographs during Victorian and Edwardian times, though during the mid twentieth century it gained another name 'the rotten bridge' as it was in a state of some disrepair. Thankfully today it is safe and sound.

Rockwood Lake, today this view would be impossible to take as the trees have matured and shrubs and climbing plants have filled the field areas, but the lake is still there. Recently renovated it is still a picturesque and tranquil place. This photograph was produced in 1904.

SQUARE WOOD RESERVOIR, DENBY DALE.

Copyright Li
Sowerby

Square Wood Reservoir in about 1940. The calm water almost denies the typhoid epidemic, which began here in 1932 causing the deaths of eleven people and serious illness to many others. The reservoir also saw the tragic death of Gordon Senior aged 16 who became tangled in the plants under the water and drowned in 1948.

View from Toby Wood Lane looking down onto the Barnsley Road or Kaye Line.

View from Toby Wood Hill Top

Miss Wood, P.O.
Denby Dale

54

WEST CLIFFE DENBY DALE

West Cliffe House, near Rockwood House, Denby Dale, circa 1900. Once home to James Henry Dewhurst, listed in the 1901 and 1912 trade directories as a Commercial Traveller, he seems to have retired by 1922 when he was noted to be living here. He was perhaps best known for being a member of the hospital committee, which was founded during the First World War. Based at the now demolished Victoria Memorial Hall the hospital provided medical facilities to convalescing soldiers during the conflict.

The road heading for West Cliffe House, leading off Wakefield Road.

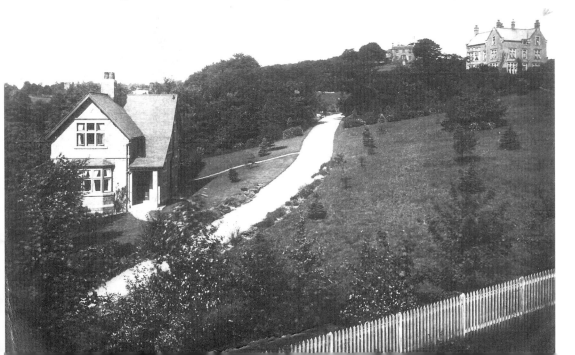

HARTCLIFFE MILLS DENBY DALE

Hartcliffe Mills, the home of well established firm Zaccheus Hinchliffe & Sons. Wakefield Road can be seen to the right and the Barnsley Road or Kaye Line can be seen to the left. Circa 1940.

A closer view of Hartcliffe Mills. Probably taken in the period between the two World Wars.

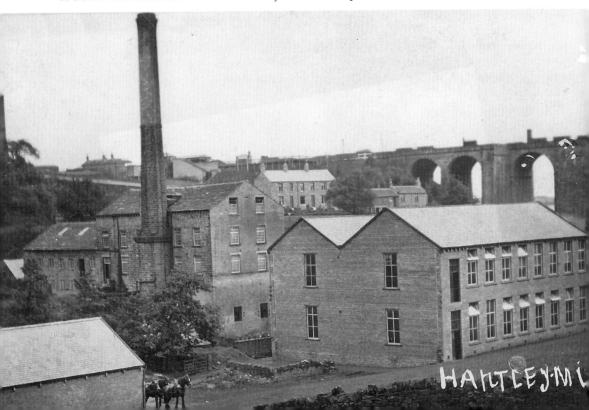

HARTLEY·MI

HARTCLIFF DENBY DALE

Strathdearne, to the top right, home to the Hinchliffe family keeps watch upon the family business. The Barnsley Road or Kaye Line can be seen to the left. Circa 1940's.

Dearne View cottages on the Barnsley Road with the solid arches of the viaduct in the background. Circa 1900.

Hartcliffe Mills and the Viaduct around 1940.

Strathdearne, home of the Hinchliffe textile manufacturing family, overlooks the mill dam and cottage.

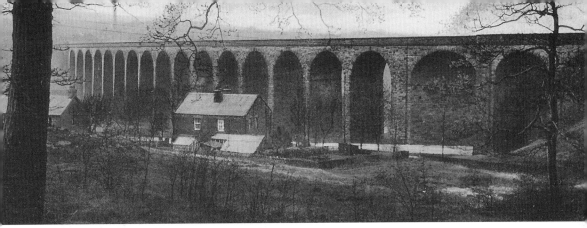

The Viaduct taken from Bank Lane around 1940.

A very early view of Hartcliffe Mills. The cottages known as Dearne View are not yet built. Circa 1890.

An early twentieth century view of the viaduct on Barnsley Road. Houses on Bank Lane can be seen behind it. The 'skew arch' of the viaduct is to the extreme right.

The Barnsley Road or Kaye Line taken from the viaduct, Hartcliffe Mills are to the right. Circa 1950.

Entrance to the continuation of the old packhorse route Bank Lane heading towards Upper Denby at the side of Hagg Wood on Barnsley Road. Only two semi-detached houses existed at this point in time. Circa 1900.

Barnsley Road, taken around 1950.

A view of the village dated around 1940. Looking over the Barnsley Road and down Church fields towards the mills of Jonas Kenyon. Note the wall, which, at this time, still separates the fields running alongside the footpath.

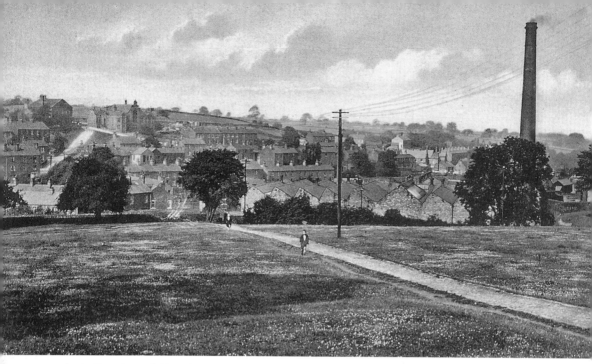

A similar view of Church Fields from the 1950's though by now the wall has gone.

Inkerman House, sometimes known as Inkerman Hall, circa 1900. Probably built by the Peace family before 1857 as a residence next to their business premises, Inkerman Mill. Two other notable local textile mill owners, John Brownhill and Sir James Peace Hinchliffe also once occupied the property.

The viaduct on entering the village from the direction of Cumberworth on the Wakefield Road. Circa 1950.

A steam train waiting at the platform at Denby Dale station. The engine shown is the 42109 built in 1949 and decommissioned and destroyed in 1965.

Denby Dale station, showing both platforms and staff during the early twentieth century.

The 'South Yorkshireman' steam train pulling into Denby Dale station. This train came into service in 1948 and ran between Bradford and London daily, calling at, amongst others, Huddersfield, Penistone, Sheffield, Nottingham and Rugby. The travel time from Bradford to London was 5½ hours. It usually had nine coaches including a restaurant car. It was decommissioned in 1960.

DENBY DALE. Nº3

Denby Dale, East of the viaduct. The premises of Naylor's and Kitson's pipe manufacturing can clearly be seen, also the long since demolished Polygon Terrace to the centre right of the photograph.

Taken from the viaduct, in the foreground is the road leading down to Hartcliffe Mill. Kitson's clay pipe manufacturing premises can be seen to the centre left on the main Wakefield Road. Adjacent to Kitson's is the long demolished row of houses known as Polygon Terrace.

A sketched postcard of the village depicting Kitson's pipe-works, Polygon Terrace and the Wesleyan Chapel.

A further sketched postcard, mainly depicting Kitson's pipe-works.

A scene of devastation at Kitson's pipe-works after a fire on 23 August 1915.

Kitson's pipe-works, showing the roofless buildings after the fire of 23 August 1915, taken from Wakefield Road.

FIRE AT DENBY DALE   AUG 23-1915

Terraced cottages on High Street. All the properties on the left are three storey with an extra upper attic room in the roof.

* * *

The following five photographs show almost the same scene from around 1900 up to the 1960's and depict only occasional changes. However, the modes of transport and style of dress certainly do alter.

Wakefield Road, showing shops to the left and the Prospect Hotel in the middle centre, taken during the Edwardian period.

The Prospect Hotel taken in 1904, the landlord at this time was Charles William Kilner.

High Street, just after the turn off to Norman Road, the Prospect Hotel to the right, circa 1910.

The centre of the village in the mid-twentieth century. Motorised vehicles have, by now, replaced the horse and cart.

Shops, including the post office, to the left in the middle of the village. The solitary Mini car parked on the road demonstrates how little traffic there used to be compared with the scene today. It also helps to date the photograph, as the Mini was not manufactured until 1959.

Norman Road. Half way down on the left is the Working Men's Club. The mills of Jonas Kenyon can be seen in the background in the middle right of the picture. Circa 1930's.

The bottom of Norman Road, showing Springfield Mills, owned by John Brownhill & Co. Hillside turns away to the right. Notice the old gas lamp to the bottom left of the photograph. Circa 1900.

The Prospect Hotel and the premises of J H Green, corn millers and grocers.

The Mathews family butchers shop on Wakefield Road. Meat can clearly be seen on display in the right hand downstairs window. The shop was founded by Joseph Mathews, originally from Shepley. His sons, Joseph, Arthur Edward and Thomas (Tom) Duckett all followed their father's profession. The photograph was taken when Tom Duckett Mathews was running the shop, around 1912.

Three young Edwardian boys pose for the camera at a row of terraced cottages off Cumberworth Lane. Circa 1910.

Dearneside Road or 'Hillside' in the foreground joins the junction of Miller Hill. The Corn Mill buildings occupy the site of what has become the Brookside housing estate. The White Hart Inn, Wesleyan Methodist Chapel and Victoria Memorial Hall can all be seen in the background. Circa 1900.

Parade and celebrations taking place at the bottom of Miller Hill in May 1935 to celebrate the Silver Jubilee of King George V.

Miller Hill. To the far right is the Primitive Methodist Chapel, which opened in 1837. The style of preaching here soon gave rise to another name for Miller Hill, which to older residents is still known colloquially as 'Ranter Hill'. The fields pictured are now covered in new housing including Revel Garth. Picture dated 1907.

MILLER HILL
DENBY DALE

The Primitive Methodist Chapel on Miller Hill, at the junction with Cuckstool Road. The building was erected in 1837 at a cost of £238. The photo is earlier than 1932, as the Sunday school has not yet been built.

Denby Dale School, which opened in 1874. Circa 1900.

This photograph is reputed to be of the workforce who were responsible for building the Denby Dale Viaduct in stone. Building work was completed in 1879 therefore the picture must date to around this time.

The cooks who created the 1896 Denby Dale Pie assemble on the stage prior to the ceremonial cutting open of the pie.

Cawthorne Young Farmers Club float heading on to Miller Hill during the 1964 Denby Dale Pie procession. The Dunkirk Inn can be seen in the background.

A closer view of the Cawthorne Young Farmers Club float during the 1964 Denby Dale Pie celebrations. The slim, handsome bloke (John Cook) sitting on the milk churn would later turn out to be heavily involved in the organisation of the Bicentennial Denby Dale Pie in 1988.

The visit of the founder of the Salvation Army, General William Booth (1829-1912) was a cause for great celebration in July 1909. This photograph must have been taken from the upper floor of the Prospect Hotel. General Booth, sporting his famous long white beard can be seen on the carriage, surrounded by local luminaries such as Zaccheus Hinchliffe, Thomas Norton, William Longley and George Herbert Norton.

Detail of the crowds listening to General Booth speak, in front of J H Green's grocers shop and corn mill on Wakefield Road in 1909.

A further detail of the assembled crowds in July 1909. Notice the Edwardian pram to the bottom right of the photograph.

The Denby Dale Women's Voluntary Service during World War Two. The WVS had been formed to act as a support for the ARP; they assisted with first aid, evacuated children and collected clothing for the needy (as pictured here) amongst many other activities. Left to right: ?, Mrs Hinchliffe, Lady Ramsden, Mrs Naylor, Mrs Longley, Mrs Wilby, ?, Miss Thackra, Mrs Kenyon, Mrs Beevors, ?.

This photograph was taken at Toby Wood Farm, Denby Dale between the Wars. The unidentified woman bottle feeding a lamb may have been a member of the Lodge family who lived and worked at the farm for many years.

The Denby Dale and District Free Church Council Garden Party at Toby Wood Farm on 27 July 1929. The Free Church Council was a voluntary association of British Nonconformist churches or chapels co-operating in religious social work.

Denby Dale Free Church Council, which was in existence between 1924-1930, pictured during a meeting at Toby Wood Farm. Sir James Peace Hinchliffe can be seen in the back row, fourth from the left. Lister Stead Peace is second from the left on the middle row.

Interior of the Victoria Memorial Hall after its adaptation to a convalescent hospital during World War One. The staff include Dr. Duncan Alistair MacGregor with his arms folded sat on one of the beds and the Matron, Miss Meadows, in the dark uniform with the white muslin cap.

The Salvation Army Band, outside the Wesleyan Methodist Chapel on Cumberworth Lane.

Some of the men of Denby Dale just prior to the beginning of World War One in 1914. Back row, left to right: H Morley, W J Lockwood, J W Marsden, A Brown, E Lockwood, F Booth, W Dalton. Seated: A Lockwood, J Lockwood, H Schofield, W Booth, J H Shaw, J Haigh.

Class One, Denby Dale Infants school in 1914.

Blanche and Ava Horn of High Street, Denby Dale, who joined the Women's Land Army in 1940 during World War Two, pictured just prior to departing by train from Huddersfield for Ashford in Kent to work as farm labourers.

Selected Historical Notes

Brownhill & Scatchard

In Denby & District II, I wrote about the foundation in 1868 of the textile mill partnership of Brownhill and Scatchard in Denby Dale. I noted that:

Very little was known of Mr Scatchard, including his first name.

And that the partnership did not seem to last for very long. A piece of this jigsaw puzzle can now be filled in thanks to The London Gazette dated 2 March 1875:

Notice is hereby given that the partnership heretofore existing between the undersigned, John Brownhill and Owen Scatchard, carrying on business at Denby Dale, near Huddersfield in the County of York, as Worsted Manufacturers, under the firm of John Brownhill and Company, is this day dissolved by mutual consent. All debts owing to and from the said firm, will be received and paid by the said John Brownhill, by whom the business will in future be carried on. Dated this 23rd day of February 1875.

What of Owen Scatchard? There are two men recorded in the nineteenth century census returns by this name. The first was born in 1855 and died in 1936. He spent all his life as a canal/river labourer and was only thirteen when the Brownhill & Scatchard partnership began – I think we can safely reject him as a possible candidate.

The other is far more promising and indeed, highly likely. Owen Scatchard was born in 1846 the son of John Scatchard (born Morley 1798 died Emley Lodge 1864). If he is our man then he moved to Heckmondwike sometime soon after the partnership ended, and would have been twenty-two years old when he went into partnership with John Brownhill who was ten years his senior. This coupled with an Owen Scatchard actually found in Denby Dale on 8 June 1872 attending a Denby Dale Wesleyan Band of Hope Society gathering, as a speaker makes the case even more compelling. We do not know the reason for the split between the pair, amicable or otherwise but we do at least now know when it happened and can give Owen Scatchard the respectability of a Christian name. He was, though, not destined for long life; he died in Heckmondwike in 1898 aged about 52.

A Denby Dale Pie in 2012?

A new Channel 5 series called The Great Northern Cookbook decided to feature Denby Dale pie as one of its items in the programme being recorded throughout summer 2012. I was contacted for help and advice in June 2012 and then again two weeks before the event. The production company had decided to attempt to replicate the Victorian 1887 pie, the one that went off and drove the eager diners away with its stench. A tall order but a fascinating challenge. A dish weighing 1½ tons was manufactured in Huddersfield at great speed and an agreement with the Denby Dale Pie company based at Denby Dale Business Park, under the shadow of the viaduct was reached for them to undertake the cooking procedure. The meat was sourced from Farmer Copleys based in Purston, near Pontefract. The desire was to try and re-create the actual ingredients from 1887 and so Farmer Copleys were asked to supply the following cut and diced meat ready for collection at 7am on Friday 17 August 2012:

435kg Beef, 50 Rabbits, 35 Pigeons, 3 Hares, 10 Grouse, 36 Chickens, 63kg of Turkey and 21 Ducks.

The Thorncliffe Farm Shop also supplied some Pork. The meat weighed in at 1.8 tons along with 300kg of potatoes topped with 185kg of short-crust pastry, which along with the weight of the dish gave a combined weight of around 3.8 tons.

Cooking was done in batches on the Friday and took ten hours, always with a keen eye on hygiene and health and safety issues. The creation of the crust was to be turned into more of a community matter and members of the production team hastily handed out leaflets and placed them in shop windows asking for volunteers to meet at the Pie Hall on Friday evening. Each volunteer was given enough pastry to make two A4 sized lids which were to be waiting at the Pie Hall on Saturday for 3pm. Luckily enough volunteers were found and they were mindful of making their efforts a little special. Children's names, the Olympic rings, dates, pictures of pies and various ingredients were decorated on the top, one including the message *Save Our Library.*

The programme was presented by actor Sean Wilson, best known for playing Martin Platt in Coronation Street for twenty years between 1985 and 2005. He also appeared in Dancing On Ice in 2006 but had also gained a high reputation from his foundation of the Saddleworth Cheese Company, which won three gongs at the 2009 British Cheese Awards.

Due to the amount of time spent in the village by the team and the very low key publicity many villagers had no idea what was going on in their midst. Most were sorry to have missed the event, but huge numbers attending would have been very difficult to cope with and incurred heavy extra costs. Ultimately, it became a friendly, local community celebration of a famous tradition, and there was nothing wrong with that.

Pastry lids were waiting by the box full at 3:00pm on Saturday 18 August, but there was no sign of the pie. A delay of about an hour was endured with good humour. Finally a tractor towing the heavily laden dish, along with Sean Wilson, made its way down Wakefield Road and into the Pie Hall car park. Lifted off by forklift truck the lid was removed and the pastry squares began to form a patchwork around the dish which was eight-foot in circumference. The general opinion was that the smell was very appetising. Once covered in pastry Sean Wilson used one of the original, Victorian ladles, usually on display in the Pie Hall to 'open' the pie. Serving began and the helpings were large and consumed heartily without cost to a happy soon to be well fed throng.

The programme was first broadcast at 8pm on Thursday 3 January 2013. The item on Denby Dale was one of four to be featured in the first episode, the others being fish and chips in Whitby, stuffed lambs' hearts in Morpeth and tripe in Liverpool.

Expectant diners in the car park at the Pie Hall await the results of the Great Northern Cookbook's efforts to re-create the 1887 pie.

Sean Wilson accompanies the 3.8 ton pie through the village before arriving at the Pie Hall.

Sean Wilson, supervising the unloading of the pie.

With the dish lid removed, villagers get their first view of the pie filling.

Sean Wilson holds up a pastry lid baked by Brooke Lynn Hodgson aged four.

All the pastry lids have now been added to the pie creating a patchwork effect.

Using a genuine Victorian Denby Dale pie ladle, Sean Wilson prepares to serve the first portion.

The next generation of 'Dalers'? Brooke Lynn Hodgson, born in Denby Dale in 2007 takes her first mouthful of Denby Dale pie, perhaps anticipating further great bakes in the future? Only time will tell.

High Hoyland

A hand drawn map showing High Hoyland in 1732.

The village of High Hoyland from the air.

A closer view of the village from the air.

The old rectory is prominent in this aerial view of High Hoyland, towards the centre left.

The Cherry Tree public house (the white building to the centre right) and old cottages from the air on High Hoyland Lane.

Hoyland Hall, built by Henry Wentworth, circa 1720 can be seen to the centre right as Church Lane swings away from High Hoyland Lane.

Hoyland Farm and Hall from the air.

An early twentieth century view of High Hoyland; Church Lane bends away to the left in the distance.

The old road-sign in the centre of High Hoyland, circa 1900.

A general view of Globe Farm, Hall Farm and Rose Cottages in 1890.

Church Lane, 1890.

Church Lane, early twentieth century.

Town Well, below the Rectory, early twentieth century.

Town End/Upperfield Lane, early twentieth century.

Pre-Second World War Council houses on Upperfield Lane as one leaves High Hoyland in the direction of Kexborough. These buildings were demolished and re-built during 1982/3.

High Hoyland from Upperfield Lane, circa 1900.

The village Post Office at Copley Fold.

The village Post Office at Copley Fold, circa 1900.

High Hoyland Post Office, early twentieth century.

Rose Cottage,
High Hoyland.

Cottages at
Hoyland Hills, on
High Hoyland
Lane, heading
down towards
Cawthorne.

Houses at Greenland, on High Hoyland Lane.

High Hoyland school, early twentieth century.

Primitive Methodist Chapel, High Hoyland, built in 1890.

Globe Farm, December 1986.

Above and Below: Globe Farm, December 1986.

Dyson's Lane,
August 1890.

The Rockwood Harriers at
High Hoyland, early
twentieth century.

Rose Cottages, 1890.

Dr Fotherly Pennel Bell (b.1820), outside High Hoyland church. He was a general practitioner in Clayton West and later became a surgeon. It was said that some of his patients paid him with eggs!

Ever ready for a photographic opportunity, one enterprising individual (Ernest Exley) climbs the road sign at the junction of Cawthorne Lane and Upperfield Lane in 1915. His friends are from left to right: George Lawson, Andrew Exley, Albert Woofenden, Harold Hutchinson and Willie Simpson. These were the only men left in the village during the First World War.

Back row, left to right: May Clarkson, Alice Simpson, Freda Drake, Mary Ellen Exley, Alice Exley, Francis Exley, Agnes Exley, Freda Lawson. The photograph was taken in 1915, probably outside the schoolhouse. The girls attended classes at the Rectory in High Hoyland once a week under the supervision of Miss Wintour and the instruction of Rev. Boxhall, who was Rector of the Parish and lived in the rectory at Clayton West. The confirmation service took place at Clayton West, the girls having first met in the church school to dress with the help of Mrs Boxhall, the Rector's wife.

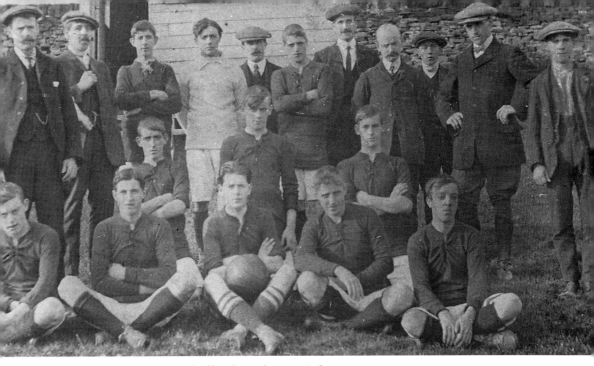

High Hoyland AFC, team and officials, early twentieth century.

Local gentleman pose at the village water trough, early twentieth century.

High Hoyland school, Class A, with their teacher Miss Drake, or Miss Duck as the children preferred to call her. Miss Drake was the headmistress and lived in the schoolhouse with her two daughters, one of whom taught at High Hoyland and the other, Miss Edith Drake, taught at Bretton. Back row, left to right: John Exley, Norman Swift, William Woofenden, James Gibson, Herbert Taylor. Middle row, left to right: Lena Woofenden, Ethel Hutchinson, Edith Ann Ball, Elsie Sunderland, Lily Woofenden, Edith Simpson. Front row, left to right: Ann Ball, Maria Simpson, Olive Clarkson, Emma Exley, Mary Ellen Exley.

High Hoyland school, Class B, 1908, with Headmistress, Miss Drake. Back row, left to right: Alan Exley, Eddie Moxon, Frank Exley, Fred Woofenden, Edgar Gore, Malcolm Gore. Middle row, left to right: Alice Simpson, Agnes Exley, Francis Exley, May Clarkson, Ernest Clarkson, Horace Hutchinson. Front row, left to right: Nora Exley, Eleanor Hutchinson, Cathleen Gore, Amy Exley, Mary Alice Clarkson, Gertrude Simpson.

School children at High Hoyland, with Headmistress, Miss Drake, around 1908. Back row, left to right: Horace Hutchinson, Alan Exley, Ernest Clarkson, Clarence Horsefield, Hubert Exley, Wilfred Exley. Middle row, left to right: Mary Elliot, Alice Exley, Freda Lawson, Alice Simpson, Agnes Exley. Front row, left to right: Violet Exley, Ethel Clarkson, Cecil Exley, Harold Clarkson, Alice Gore. The girl on the tricycle is Freda Drake, who was Miss Drake's niece and lived with her at the schoolhouse.

School children, High Hoyland, taken just before the First World War: Back row, left to right: Joe Burton, Harry Smith, Arthur Exley, Noah Cowling. Middle row, left to right: Miss Naylor (the new Headmistress), Margaret Broadhead, Venus Firth, Horace Exley, Albert Exley, Vincent Gore, Jack Clarkson, Edgar Clarkson, Sarah Senior, Alice Gill, Miss Drake (the former Headmistress). Front row, left to right: Hilda Smith, Beaumont Firth, Mary Moxon, Eric Lockwood, Hilda Smith, Leonard Armstrong, Florence Senior, Joel Firth, Bertha Exley, Stanley Lockwood, Betty Exley. Seated: Arthur Gill, Norman Lockwood.

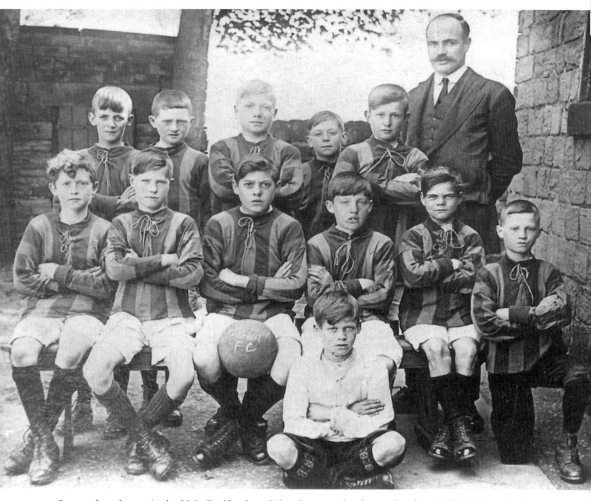

Soon after the arrival of Mr Bedford as Schoolmaster he formed a football club for the boys. This was received with great enthusiasm but unfortunately, enthusiasm alone was not enough to win matches and sadly the school team never did win a match. Their opponents were the local schools and many of the matches were played in the field behind the school. Back row, left to right: Vincent Gore, Albert Exley, Ernest Cudworth, Edgar Clarkson, Charles Lockwood. Middle row, left to right: Jack Clarkson, Horace Exley, Harry Burton, Harry Smith, Mars Firth, Arthur Exley. Seated: Joe Burton.

High Hoyland school pupils in around 1923. Back row, left to right: Fred Bedford (Headmaster), Jack Clarkson, Horace Exley, Ernest Cudworth, Arthur Exley, Harry Smith, Edgar Clarkson, Fred Cowling. Middle row, left to right: Bob Hill, Vincent Gore, Annie Lockwood, Venus Firth, Annie Gill, Sarah Senior, Alice Gill, Noah Cowling, Charlie Lockwood. Front row, left to right: Arthur Exley, Joe Burton, Arthur Gill, Cyril Exley, Florence Senior, Fred Exley, Hilda Smith, Joel Firth, Bertha Exley, Betty Exley, Kathleen Exley.

High Hoyland Chapel held its first Field Day during September 1948, in Norton's field, opposite the Globe Inn. There was no band present but a fancy dress competition was held with many villagers taking part. The competition was judged by Mrs F W Hewis of Clayton West. This photograph was taken in front of the Globe Inn. Competitors included: Mrs Graham, Margaret Howard, Mrs Harry Morley, Roger Fisher, Christine Exley, Margaret Allot, Beryl Fisher, Jennifer Bowman, Valerie Fisher, May Morley, Mary Graham and John and Richard Graham.

The Festival of Britain was held in 1951 and High Hoyland Chapel decided to have a Sunday school Queen. The third Field Day was held in June 1951 and Maureen Hill aged fourteen was crowned the Sunday school Queen by Mrs J H Fisher of Skelmanthorpe who was a Sunday school teacher and pianist. Maureen and her family lived at Dean Hill at Cawthorne. The photograph shows Maureen being crowned by Mrs Fisher.

High Hoyland Chapel, Sunday school concert, December 1951. Back row, left to right: Malcolm Bowman, John Wood, June Mannifield. Front row, left to right: Michael Gore, Jennifer Bowman, Denise Loukes, Christine Exley, D Mannifield, Pat Morley, Barbara Gore.

High Hoyland Sunday school concert 1951. Stood, left to right: Barbara Gore, Christine Exley. Seated, left to right: Jennifer Bowman, Denise Loukes, Pat Morley.

Clayton West Band, leading the procession from the Chapel around the village to Morley's Croft, as part of the 1951 celebrations.

High Hoyland Chapel, Sunday school Field Day, June 1955. Betty Metcalfe is the Queen; her attendants were Janet Gorthorpe, Glenise Truelove, Jeanette Milner, Dorothy Mannifield and Catherine Lumby. June Mannifield was reserve Queen, her attendants were: Patricia Morley, Sandra Jessop, Margaret Jessop, Ann Jessop, Helen Lumby and Colin Thickett was the cushion bearer.

In 1955 the High Hoyland Sunday school scholars won the shield for the Scripture Examination. This photograph shows all the successful pupils with the shield.

The new Sunday school Queen flanked by former holders of the position, including: Helen Lumby, Sandra Jessop, Dorothy Mannifield, Betty Metcalfe, June Mannifield and Christine Exley.

High Hoyland Chapel, Sunday school Queen, 1961. The retiring Queen crowns Margaret Jessop who was the last Sunday school Queen.

To mark the Silver Jubilee of King George V in 1935 a large bonfire was built to celebrate the occasion in High Hoyland. Money had been collected around the villages and a marquee was erected in the Croft (the field below Croft Cottage). Local farmer, Mr Elliot from Hall Farm lent his horse and cart to fetch the wood for the bonfire and Beanland's of Clayton West provided the skips and tyres. Games and competitions were held in the afternoon followed by tea in the marquee, catering being undertaken by Harold Brook. Everyone then made their way to Beacon Field for the fireworks and lighting of the bonfire.

Included in this photograph are: Wilfred Hutchinson, Harry Smith, Willie Moxon, Albert Exley, Wilfred Exley, George Lawson, Joe Barker, Albert Mitchell and Andrew Exley.

𝕾elected 𝕳istorical 𝕹otes

The following Manorial records have never been published before and complement other documents that have been included in previous works.

Resolutions of Court Leet and Court Burse of High Hoyland – held 14 October 1652.
A plaint is laid that Mathew Chapel has not removed his dunghill and rubbish from before Thomas Syke's window. Fine 3s4d.

Robert Smith, Parish Constable for not keeping watch and ward, according to stature. Fine 7d.

Robert Smith, Parish Constable for not keeping due Common Pound in repair 'as it ought'. Fine 7d.

Mary Walton, for her crafty grazing of more sheep on the Common than she ought to put on. She is in mercy. Fine 1s.

Sara Ellis and John Ellis, for putting on the Common more horses than they ought. They are all in mercy. Fine 7s.

Court Leet and Great Court Burse held 18 October 1664 in 'Ye Manor House' at High Hoyland.
A plaint is laid that all persons shall 'ring their swine' and keep them ringed till Candlemass next and then to yoke them and keep them yoked until the next court under pain of every default. Fine 3s4d.

Also that Haigh Lane be repaired by the jurymen, and it shall commence before the last day of this instant November under paine for every default. Fine 5s.

Also that no persons shall make way over a close called 'Deffer Foote' under paine for further default. Fine 5s.

Also that Town-end gate in High Hoyland leading up to the church to be made sufficient before the tenth day of March next. In paine for further default. Fine 10s.

Also plaint is laid that Thomas Earnshaw and Christopher Wofenden make their wall between the Town Gate and Christopher Wofenden's house end before Martinmass-daye next, and so keep it from time to time in repair under paine of default. Fine 3s1d.

We also lay in Paine that all persons who have any ground adjoining upon the highway between Little Bretton and High Hoyland Church shall cut and switch their hedges where they are in any way an annoyance before the tenth day of May next, upon default. Fine 5s.

At the Court Leet of Our Sovereign Lord Charles II and the Court Baron of Sir Mathew Wentworth, Holden at Manor House in High Hoyland 23 October 1666.
A plaint is laid that no manner of persons shall make waye over the land of Thomas Holden at Shuffroyd, contrary to the usual waye. On default fine 1s.

A plaint is laid that Edward Nicholes make the Northfield Close Gate before Candlemass Day next, and so keep it in repair from time to time, upon paine of every default. 2s.

A plaint is laid that William Hearmand and Thomas Bramall make a gate at Hoyland Town-end leading to the Church and keep it in repair, upon paine of every default 5s.

A plaint is laid that no persons shall make other way across Well Close and High Close in occupation of William Dyson, in paine 10d.

We find that Thomas Smith and John Appleyard and the occupiers of the land they now possess have maintained the Gate that goes into Cross Gates Close at an equal change; but that Thomas Smith and John Appleyard repair the stoops belonging to the said gate and order them to be repaired in the same manner, under paine of default 6s8d.

High Hoyland – Rent Roll – Martinmass, 11 November 1677.

Name	£	s	d
Joshua Worall	7	3	7
Robert Smith	3	10	0
Richard Ellis	1	19	6
Mathew Hill	8	10	0
Widow Pollard	1	5	0
William Exley	2	13	4
Richard Langley	2	14	0
Robert More	14	0	3
Thomas Smith	1	0	0
Widow Pollard	7	13	8
Edward Howlden	0	10	6
George Howlden	2	15	0
East Sickes	8	2	8
Christopher Wollenden	1	10	6
Joseph Howlden	1	15	0

Mathew Hayley	0	2	6
Joshua Hayley	0	3	4
Thomas Raynor	0	2	6
Widow Crawshaw	0	2	6
William Dreighton for Land in Clayton	0	2	6
Mathew Howlden	0	0	4

Henry Wentworth, builder of High Hoyland Hall.

High Hoyland was once a part of the extensive manors and lands owned by the Burdet family of Denby. During the reign of King Charles II, the Birthwaite branch of the family sold the estates at High Hoyland to the Wentworth family of Bretton (for the details regarding this see Denby & District V1, chapter 3). The Burdets had never built a Hall at High Hoyland though they did hold Manorial Courts there from at least the early fourteenth-century. Henry Wentworth, a member of the Bretton family is widely regarded to have been responsible for High Hoyland Hall's construction in around 1720. He lived here until his death in 1736. The Hall was grade II listed in 1968.

The Last Will of Henry Wentworth of High Hoyland Hall 1736.

In the name of God Amen, I Henry Wentworth of High Hoyland in this County of York, gentleman, being weak in bodily health but of sound mind and understanding do make ordain and declare this my last will and testament in writing in manner and form following. First I give and bequeath unto Mary and Dorothy my sisters each of them £200 to be paid them respectively within six months after my death and also the sum of £20 a pair to buy them mourning withall to be paid them within one month after my death and I do give Mrs Elizabeth Wentworth £500 to be paid her within twelve months after my death and I do give to John Taylor parish clerk £5 and to Phillip Witton £20 and to Elizabeth Firth and Elizabeth my other maid servant each of them £5 to be paid them respectively within six months after my decease and I do give and bequeath to the poor of the parish of High Hoyland the sum of £5 to be distributed to them at the discretion of my executor and the church wardens and overseers of the poor and I do hereby give and bequeath unto Pheobe Hooksbank all my household goods, cattle, corn, hay, implements of husbandry and stone belonging my messuage and dwelling house, farm and premises which I hold by lease from Sir William Wentworth for a certain term of years of which there is to expire seventeen years or thereabouts and I do hereby also give the said messuage, farm and premises for and during the remainder of the said term in the said lease unto the said Phoebe Hooksbank if she shall so long live and after her death I give and surrender the said messuage's, farm and premises unto the said Sir William Wentworth, his heir and assigns all the rest of my goods and chattels so all and personal estate I give and bequeath unto Sir William Wentworth and I hereby make, constitute and appoint the said Sir William (sole executor) of this my last will and testament hereby revoking all other wills by me formally made. I witness whereby I the said Henry Wentworth testator have hereunto set my hand and seal this twenty fourth day of March in the fourth year of the Reign of our Sovereign Lord George the Second, by the Grace of God of Great Britain, France and Ireland, King, Defender of the Faith and in the year of our Lord 173 and 6 the writing of Henry Wentworth sealed, signed, published and declared by the said testator after interlineations of several words in five several places in the presence of us subscribed our names in his presence as Witnesses thereto: Bryan Allott, Ann Haigh, William Oates.

Education in High Hoyland.

The National Society for Education in Church Principals was founded in 1811, which by 1831 was responsible for the education of nearly half a million children. It was founded by Andrew Bell of the National Society and Joseph Lancaster, a Quaker for the British and Foreign School Society who had tested this system and found that it worked in Madras hence 'the Madras System'. A meeting was held at High Hoyland in 1816 for the purpose of establishing a school for 'the instruction of boys' for Clayton West and High Hoyland under the Chairmanship of Thomas Wentworth Beaumont. The meeting decided to follow the Madras system

> *and in subordination to the National Society; and that the moral and religious instruction therein conveyed be uniformity with the doctrine and discipline of the established church.*

Thomas Richard Beaumont was appointed President. Walter Spencer Stanhope, Thomas Wentworth Beaumont, Joseph Kay, Benjamin Micklethwaite, Charles Stringer and the Rector of High Hoyland were appointed Managers. Rev. Christopher Bird was appointed Treasurer and William Jackson the Secretary.

A meeting of the Trustees in January 1820 made a call for more funds as there were none to meet the extra costs of the school beyond that of the Masters £30 salary.

The school relied heavily upon its benefactors. In 1886 John E Kaye can be found donating £10 in May towards the building of a porch at the school and a further £10 in September.

In 1932 the Board of Education had deemed that High Hoyland School was unnecessary as adequate arrangements existed at Clayton West at Kaye's Council School and closure swiftly followed.

Methodist Chapel at High Hoyland.

Three hundred square yards of land was donated by W B Beaumont MP of Bretton Hall for the purposes of erecting a Methodist chapel. The estimated cost of the building was £300, which was completed and opened in 1890. The dedication sermon was given by the Rev. J Ayrton of Belle Vue, Wakefield. The chapel closed after the last service was held there on 5 April 1987.

Archaeological Dig at High Hoyland.

Barnsley archaeological group commenced investigations at High Hoyland in October 1982. A field-walking programme was carried out until December, which brought to light such finds as flint scrapers dating to the late Stone Age. Pottery was also collected and included some medieval shards. Clay pipes, some coins, musket balls, spindle whorl and a fragment of painted plaster were also recovered. Prior to this investigation quantities of molten slack had been recovered providing evidence of Iron Age activity upon the site. In January 1983 a preliminary investigation was begun at the side of the church to try to ascertain the whereabouts of the earlier medieval and perhaps Saxon buildings.

The first tenth century chapel had been abandoned by the time of the Norman Conquest but was revived in stone by the late twelfth century. In the fifteenth century the church was re-roofed with lead and several perpendicular windows were inserted. The tower was rebuilt in 1662 and the rest of the church in the late eighteenth century. Further re-building took place during 1904-1908.

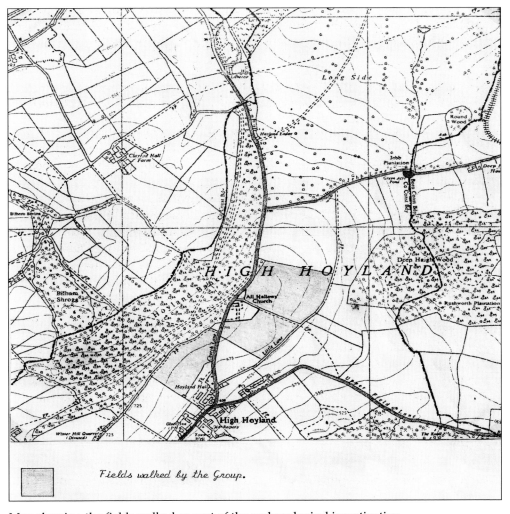

Map showing the fields walked as part of the archaeological investigation.

Fragments of clay pipes found during field walking.

High Hoyland Church, prior to re-building during 1904-1908.

High Hoyland Church during re-building, the nave was entirely replaced during this period.

High Hoyland Church after re-building had completed in 1908.

ORDER OF SERVICE

FOR THE

RE-OPENING

OF

All Hallows Church,

HIGH HOYLAND,

AFTER RESTORATION,

And for the Consecration of the New Portion
of the Churchyard,

BY THE BISHOP OF WAKEFIELD,

ON SATURDAY, MAY 9TH, 1908.

At THREE p.m.

We wait for Thy loving kindness, O God, in the midst of Thy Temple.

W. H. MILNES LTD., Radcliffe Works, WAKEFIELD.

Order of Service produced for the ceremonial re-opening of High Hoyland Church in May 1908.

Initially excavation began at the East Side of the church but this was quickly abandoned when it was realised that the foundations of the present church probably covered earlier work. Excavation then began on the North side, which uncovered part of the nineteenth century wall. A skeleton was also found here, most likely having being disturbed during previous re-building work. The remains were of a male dating to approximately the fifteenth century. An extreme curve in the spine of the skeleton suggested that he was probably a hunchback during his life. A further, older wall was also discovered, this one dating to the thirteenth century church. A buttress was uncovered, probably one of at least three or four more in a line. A skeleton was also found next to the buttress, this one that of a middle-aged woman who may have suffered from rickets. This skeleton was removed for further examination. At some point during her life the woman had broken her leg and although it had healed it had not stretched which meant one leg was about an inch shorter than the other and that she would have walked with a limp. Another skeleton, that of a child, was found near to the thirteenth century wall near what was thought to be another buttress. Further skeletons were found in the foundations of the thirteenth century wall.

The remains of the fifteenth-century male hunchback discovered by the nineteenth century wall during archaeological excavations in 1983.

The nineteenth-century wall and remains of the male hunchback.

The thirteenth-century buttress found during excavations in 1983.

The thirteenth-century wall unearthed during the 1983 excavations.

The jumbled remains of the middle aged woman who may have suffered from rickets found next to the thirteenth century wall.

The skull of the middle aged woman dating from the thirteenth century, as it was found in the grave in 1983.
Inset: This button was found with the remains of the middle aged thirteenth century woman.

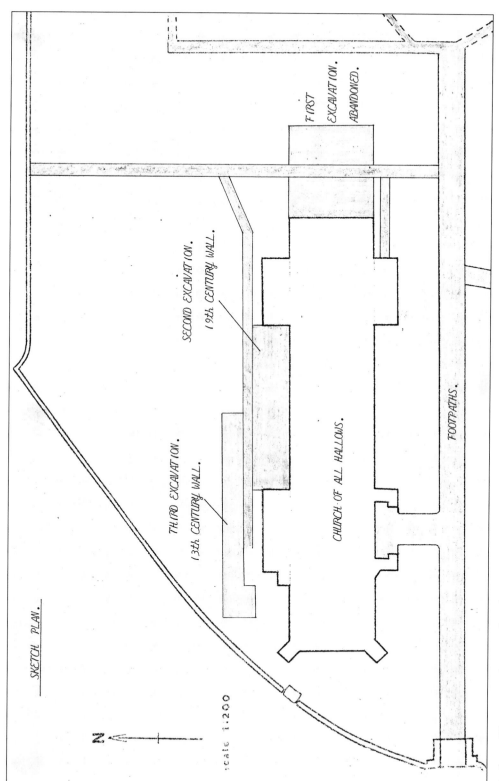

A plan of the excavations undertaken in 1983 showing the two earlier walls discovered by the team.

Metal Detecting Find

A further archaeological artefact was discovered in High Hoyland in around 2002. This find was a seal matrix (or die) of the late twelfth or early thirteenth century. The seal would have been used by its owner to make an impression into hot wax to seal a document. It was 28mm in diameter, made of lead and inscribed in Latin, which was translated as *'The Seal of Adela Hollan*(d)*'*. The seal featured a bird (possibly a sparrow) walking to the left. The name Adela is Germanic and she seems to have lived at around the same time as Adam de Hoyland who was Lord of the Manor of Hoyland and alive between 1204 and 1240. To have had her own seal Adela must have been a high ranking individual. It might also be speculated that Adela and Adam are very similar looking names, Adam married Maud de Notton therefore Adela was not his wife, could the translation be slightly wrong and here we have physical evidence for the existence of an early Lord of Hoyland?

The Globe Inn

During the Middle Ages a timber and plaster building stood upon the site later to become The Globe Inn or The Cherry Tree as it is known today. Its sign was that of a bush hung at the end of a long pole to advertise its amenities to travellers. The induction of Alexander de Vaux as rector of High Hoyland by the Archbishop in 1281 saw the pair accommodated

A representation of the Globe Inn as it may have looked in 1893 by B Lawrence (1983).

The Globe Inn, circa 1900.

in that year at the Inn as the rectory was in such a ruinous condition. The first knowledge of an actual name for the Inn is during the eighteenth century when it was known as The Cherry Tree, possibly derived from the orchards behind it. By 1830 it had become known as The Shoulder of Mutton and then, in 1870 as The Globe. As an aside, the pinfold (used for impounding stray animals) was adjacent to the Inn.

In order to defray expenses to the erection of a tower at the church and cake and ale feast held on Whit-Monday 1662, the ale was brewed by the churchwardens in the brewhouse attached to the Inn. Refreshment was also provided here for those who attended the Manorial Court. The Overseers of the Poor met at the Inn to allocate relief and provide tuition for local orphans and poor children. The churchwardens likewise to settle their accounts, elect the constable and highway surveyor each Easter at the annual vestry. In 1816 the leading Gentlemen of the district met at the Inn under the Chairmanship of Sir Thomas Wentworth to found a school for all the boys in Clayton and Hoyland, which survived until 1935. The Steward of Bretton (on behalf of his Lord) collected rents from his Masters tenants here half yearly and then provided dinner in what is now the taproom. For over seven hundred years an Inn has stood upon this site, the Cherry Tree (as it is known today) remains the focal point of the village of High Hoyland.

The Globe Inn, around 1910.

The Globe Inn, circa 1950's.

Arthur Cooper, landlord of the Globe Inn during the 1950's and 60's outside the front door. Mr Cooper was a World War Two veteran, having served as Chief Petty Officer and Master at Arms on HMS Sheffield, a cruiser which won twelve honours to become one of the most illustrious warships of the conflict. After the war he served as a Police Constable at Wombwell, Mapplewell and Kexborough before taking over the Globe Inn for thirteen years. He eventually moved away from the area, spending his retirement in Dorset.

The Globe Inn during the 1960's.

The Cherry Tree, formerly the Globe Inn, circa 1980's.

The Cherry Tree on High Hoyland Lane, circa 1980's.

Modern day aerial view of the Cherry Tree Inn and car park.

Joseph Wolff

Doctor Joseph Wolff was born in 1795 in Germany and became a missionary. He married Lady Georgina Walpole,, the daughter of the 2nd Earl of Oxford and bore them a son christened Henry Drummond Wolff (later Sir Henry). Doctor Wolff's missionary work had taken him into the Middle East and North Africa, countries including Palestine, Egypt, Afghanistan and India, though he was not universally welcomed. He was bastinadoed in Turkey (beaten and whipped on the soles of his feet), in Turkistan he was flogged and in Abyssinia he was horse whipped. Doctor Wolff was a man of very strong character and faith.

In 1838 at the age of 43, Joseph arrived in High Hoyland, appointed as Curate at the Church during the long incumbency of the absentee Rector, Christopher Bird. His appointment lasted just four years before he undertook a quest, perhaps more dangerous than any he had experienced before.

The British Government had sent a certain Colonel Charles Stoddart to Bukhara (modern Uzbekistan) to offer the Emir military assistance against an expected Russian attack in 1838. Stoddart behaved with such arrogance that the Emir had him incarcerated in the 'siah chah' or black well. The well was actually a deep pit filled with tics, snakes and reptiles that lived off human flesh when denied their usual offal. After being hauled in and out of the pit for a year, Stoddart was then forced to watch his own grave being dug before him and was offered the choice of becoming a Muslim or being burned alive. Unsurprisingly by this time he undertook conversion. A very belated British rescue operation was undertaken led by Captain Arthur Conolly. Unfortunately Conolly's arrival

Arthur Conolly (left) and Charles Stoddart (right) who were executed in 1842 after imprisonment in the snake pit in Bukhara.

in Bukhara coincided with the massacre of British forces in the mountains South of Kabul by the Emir and he was forced to join Stoddart in the pit. They remained here until 1842.

Joseph Wolff had become aware of the plight of these two men and so determined to try to negotiate their release He set off from High Hoyland to Bukhara with no official support for his mission, though a 'Stoddart & Conolly' committee did raise funds for his expenses. After a torrid journey Wolff was made aware of rumours suggesting that both of the British soldiers had been executed and that if he entered the city he would suffer the same fate. He was also warned that:

> *He would be met by horsemen carrying chains to bind him and knives to cut off his head.*

As he neared the city the horsemen duly arrived but he was astonished when he found that they carried only offerings of food and drink. He entered the city and at first was treated well but no one would tell him anything of the two men he searched for.

The plain fact was that the rumours were true, both had been executed on 17 June 1842 before Wolff had even left High Hoyland and he was now placed in the same pit the soldiers had occupied before their demise. Wolff was offered death if he would not become a Muslim but he refused and prepared for his own execution. Unexpectedly the head of the Russian mission to Bukhara and the Persian Ambassador combined to effect Wolff's release from the Emir and so he was allowed to leave and make his way home. He did not return to High Hoyland but lived out the remainder of his days as an eccentric but well loved Vicar of a Somerset village, and died in 1862.

Rev. Fitzgerald Thomas Wintour
Vicar of High Hoyland 1867-1898

If the story of one single individual from High Hoyland deserved to be told in full it would have to be that of Fitzgerald Thomas Wintour. Arriving in High Hoyland at a time when religious attitudes were changing rapidly, he was an energetic man who oversaw and affected these changes. He was also a man with some fascinating family links. Amongst them we find the current editor of Vogue Magazine, a Major General, a Navy Captain during the First World War and the General Manager of the Great Exhibition.

We will begin by examining his forbears before continuing on with his achievements and those of his children.

Fitzgerald Thomas Wintour was born in 1829, the son of the Rev. Fitzgerald Wintour and Jane Elizabeth Dayrell. The family can be found in the 1851 census returns for Barton, South West of Nottingham.

1851 Census Return for Barton, Nottinghamshire.

Name	Age	Born	Occupation	Place of Birth
Fitzgerald Wintour	48	1803	Rector of Barton	Windsor
Jane Elizabeth Wintour	46	1805	Rector's Wife	Shudy Camps, Cambs.
Fitzgerald Thomas Wintour	21	1829		Grousden Parva, Cambs.
Mildred C Wintour	18	1833		Barton, Notts.
Cordelia Wintour	16	1835		Barton, Notts.
Robert C Wintour	9	1842	Scholar at home	Barton, Notts.
John Wright	46	1805	House Servant	Helion, Bumpstead, Essex
Elizabeth Coxon	31	1820	Ladies Maid	Spondon, Derbyshire.
Mary Clower	34	1817	Cook	Brumcote, Notts.
Hannah Glover	29	1822	Housemaid	Radford, Notts.

Fitzgerald Wintour was the Rector of Barton from 1829 until his death in 1863. As can be seen, this was a family of some means. Jane Elizabeth Dayrell was the daughter of Marmaduke Dayrell who was the son of Sir Robert Lawley Bt, who had married Jane Bielby Thompson who was the cousin of the famous soldier, General Woolfe. General James Woolfe (1727-1759) was famous for his part in the victory over the French at Quebec in Canada, though he died at the height of the battle it paved the way to the capture of Montreal, thereby ending French control of the country.

Rev. Fitzgerald Wintour was the son of Henry Wintour (born 1777) and we can trace his lineage back a little further with a genealogical table as shown on page 138.

The earliest member of the family currently known was Thomas Winter (note the variant spelling) of Penrith in Cumbria. Born in around 1660 he was noted to be a merchant and married a woman we know only as Mary. He made a provision prior to his death in order that his wife and only son, Thomas should be able to live at the family home at Ellerbeck which also included barns, stables and orchards. Thomas signed his will in 1687 and it was proved in 1689. His wife, Mary, went on to re-marry one William Morland, though this marriage also ended abruptly with his death in 1698 in Kirkby Kendal.

Thomas and Mary's son, Thomas Winter can be found in a marriage settlement dated 1716. Described as an ironmonger, the document details the family home at Ellerbeck and other property, which was to become home to his wife, Anne Forth, the eldest daughter of Lancelot Forth. Lancelot served twice as the Mayor of Kendal (in 1684 and 1708) and was also an Alderman. Thomas followed his father in law and was unanimously elected as a town burgess, later becoming an Alderman (he resigned in 1735) and served as Mayor for

The Wintour Family

Thomas Winter -1689

[1] Mary -1742

[1] Mary -1742

William Morland (2nd marriage) 1653 - 1698

Rev. Thomas Fitzgerald -1752

Lancelot Forth

Anne Forth

Ann Fitzgerald 1734 - 1778

Thomas Winter -1746

Thomas Winter 1723 -

Forth Winter 1724 - 1778

Thomas Wintour 1755 -

Charles Forth Wintour 1756 - 1817

Mary 1755 - 1804

Frances Wintour 1763 - 1787

? Leicester

Catherine Wintour 1764 - 1764

George Stephenson Wintour 1769 - 1839

Louisa Hillier 1787 - 1858

Rev. Henry Wintour 1777 - 1804

Mildred -1836

Sir Robert Lawley Bt. 1736 - 1793

Jane Thompson 1743 - 1816

Anna Mildred Wintour 1804 -

George Healey

10 children

Marmaduke Dayrell -1821

Mildred Rebecca Lawley

Jane Elizabeth Dayrell 1805 -

Rev. Fitzgerald Wintour 1803 - 1863

Charles Henry Wintour 1802 -

Louisa Anne Wintour 1822 - 1829

Charles Forth Wintour 1824 -

Charlotte

William Henry Wintour 1827 - 1829

Louisa Julia Wintour 1860 -

Kendal in 1719. The couple had at least two sons, Thomas and Forth Winter who both became solicitors.

Forth Winter (named to perpetuate his mother's maiden name) was born in about 1724 and left Cumbria to enter the Middle Temple in 1741. Middle Temple is one of the four Inns of Court exclusively entitled to call their members to the English Bar as barristers; the others being the Inner Temple, Gray's Inn and Lincoln's Inn. It is located in the wider Temple area of London, near the Royal Courts of Justice, and within the City of London. Forth became a solicitor based in Pall Mall and married Anne Fitzgerald in 1751 in Wotton, Surrey. Anne was the daughter of Rev. Thomas Fitzgerald who conducted the wedding, though he died a year later. Here we have the reason for the repeated re-use of the Fitzgerald name down through later generations. The couple had at least six children, including Henry, the Grandfather of Rev. Thomas Fitzgerald Wintour.

Before we consider Henry we can examine a little of the lives of his siblings, two of whom made their careers in the British Navy. The family burial site, surrounded by railings in the churchyard at Sundridge, near Sevenoaks, Kent is enlightening:

On south side:
Charles Forth Wintour, Esq. of the Royal Navy died 5 August 1817 aged 61 years. William Henry, aged 15 months and Louisa Anne aged 7 years died March 1829, children of George Stephenson and Louisa Wintour. In the same vault rest the mortal remains of George Stephenson Wintour, a Commander in the Royal Navy, father of the above. He died at Rochester June 16 1839 aged 70 years.

East end:
Charles and George Wintour, Officers of the Royal Navy and only surviving sons of Forth and Anne Wintour. On their return to their native parish from various services in foreign countries ordered this tomb to be erected as a memorial of love and pious duty towards these most honoured and most affectionate relatives.

North side:
To the memory of Mary Wintour, wife of Charles Forth Wintour, only issue of William Scawen, Esq. late of Woodcott Lodge in the County of Surrey, who died 16 March 1804 aged 49 years. Also to the memory of Frances Leicester, youngest daughter of Forth and Ann Wintour, who died 16 January 1787 aged 24 years. Beneath this stone rest the mortal remains of Anne, wife of the late Forth Wintour Esq., formerly resident at Ovenden in this parish. Only daughter and heiress of the Revd. Thomas Fitzgerald, late Rector of Wotton and Abinger in Surrey, who died 6 October 1778 aged 44 years. Also Catherine Wintour who died 4 February 1764, an infant.

Charles Forth Wintour can be found as a Lieutenant in the Navy 1794 and it is known that George Stephenson Wintour served under Captain Richard Burgess at the Battle of Camperdown in 1797 aboard the Ardent. Wintour was at this time a Second Lieutenant in this battle between the British fleet and the Dutch allies of Napoleon in which the British won a resounding victory. George Stephenson Wintour retired from the Navy as a Commander in 1824. He had also become a Naval Knight of Windsor.

Henry Wintour was the younger brother to the two seafaring siblings mentioned above. He was born in 1777 and attended Eton college and Christ Church, Oxford where he attained his BA in 1800. Whilst at Oxford, Henry became friends with the literary historian Henry Hallam. After graduating Reverend Henry became a prebendary of St. Paul's cathedral. A prebend is the form of benefice held by a prebendary, and historically the stipend attached to it was usually drawn from specific sources in the income of the cathedral's estates. When attending cathedral services, prebendaries sit in particular seats, usually at the back of the choir stalls, known as prebendal stalls. Henry married a woman we know only as Mildred who bore him three children, including Fitzgerald Wintour, who was to be the father of Thomas Fitzgerald Wintour of High Hoyland. Soon after the birth of Anna Mildred, his only daughter, Henry died from tuberculosis aged only 27, which left his wife and three children in a precarious financial situation. Mildred Wintour was reduced to living on charity. Harry Hallam afforded her some financial assistance on at least one occasion but the self pitying letters she often sent to him, hint that further help would have been more than welcome. The family did survive and Anna Mildred grew up to be described by a contemporary as 'setting all Cambridge on fire with her beauty'.

Anna was born in 1804 and drew many admirers including Harry Hallam's son, Arthur and James Milnes Gaskell. Hallam was an old family friend and Gaskell met her through Hallam. Letters and poems written by the two men relate clearly their love for her. Whilst wintering in Italy with her mother and maternal aunt, Anna and Gaskell spent time together, indeed Gaskell's private journals of his time in Italy are devoted, almost entirely, to her. Neither man was successful in their pursuit of Anna, Hallam eventually got over her but died at the early age of just 22. Gaskell made a successful marriage but always remained fond of her and left her a pension when he died, indeed Gaskell's daughter, Isabel Milnes Gaskell married Anna's nephew and the future Rector of High Hoyland Thomas Fitzgerald Wintour as we shall see.

Anna eventually married a Yorkshire squire, Colonel George Healey in 1834 and had ten children, none of which survived to maturity, she died on 30 March 1880, aged 76 and was buried at Middleton Tyas, near Richmond, North Yorkshire.

At this point it might be interesting to speculate about the possibility of a connection between our Wintour family and the one connected with one of the most infamous events in British history. We have noted above that the family surname was originally spelt Winter not Wintour. This change seems to have occurred at around the time of Forth Winter's death. Thomas Winter, Forth's eldest son entered Lincoln's Inn in London in 1773, attained his BA in 1775 still using the spelling Winter but when he achieved his MA in 1779 the spelling had changed to Wintour. This change could simply have been an affectation created by the family's growing social awareness. The fact that it was adopted by all the family and the variant spelling of the surname that they decided to use may point to them having discovered a link to an old family of the same name that perhaps they either admired or may have been related to.

The Wintour family of Huddington Court.

Robert Wintour (1568-1606) and Thomas Wintour (1571-1606) were the sons of George Wintour and Jane Ingleby of Huddington Court, Worcestershire.

Robert and Thomas were members of what became known as the Gunpowder Plot, a failed conspiracy to assassinate King James I. Both men were related to other co-conspirators, such as a half-brother, John Wintour and the ring-leader, Robert Catesby, whose sister, Elizabeth may have married Thomas Wintour in a secret Catholic ceremony. Robert Wintour had made an important dynastic alliance by marrying Gertrude Talbot, daughter of Sir John Talbot of Grafton, the heir presumptive to the earldom of Shrewsbury.

Briefly, Thomas Wintour, an intelligent and well-educated man, fluent in several languages and trained as a lawyer chose instead to become a soldier. He fought in France and central Europe. By 1600 he had a change of heart and became a Catholic even travelling to Spain of behalf of England's oppressed Catholics to enlist that country's support for a rebellion in England. Thomas's efforts came to nothing as a peace settlement was close between the two nations. In 1604 he joined with Robert Catesby who planned to restore Catholicism to England by killing the King and inciting a popular revolt, installing the King's daughter, Princess Elizabeth as titular Queen. On a further trip to plead with the Spanish, Thomas returned to England in the company of a certain Guido Fawkes (1570-1606). Robert Wintour, a devout Catholic who had inherited Huddington Court joined with his brother and Catesby in 1604.

The plot began to unravel following the delivery of an anonymous letter to William Parker, 4th Baron Monteagle, warning him to stay away from Parliament. The Wintour brothers and Catesby confronted Monteagle's brother-in-law, the recently recruited Francis Tresham and threatened to kill him but Tresham persuaded them of his innocence in the matter. At this stage, Thomas asked Catesby to abandon the scheme but Catesby was determined.

The plotters had secured the lease to an undercroft beneath the House of Lords, and Fawkes was placed in charge of the gunpowder they stockpiled there. Prompted by the receipt of the anonymous letter, the authorities searched Westminster Palace during the early hours of 5 November, and found Fawkes guarding the explosives. Over the next few days, he was questioned and tortured, and eventually he broke. Immediately before his execution on 31 January, Fawkes jumped from the scaffold where he was to be hanged and broke his neck, thus avoiding the agony of the mutilation of being hung, drawn and quartered that followed.

Following this Thomas fled to Robert's home, Huddington Court. Catesby and most of the other conspirators spent two days attempting to incite rebellion across the Midlands. With an ever-diminishing group of supporters they finally settled at Holbeche House in Staffordshire and waited for the Government forces to arrive. Thomas, by now re-integrated into the group was shot in the shoulder and captured in the ensuing fight. Robert Wintour evaded capture until January 1606. The brothers were tried on 27 January 1606 and hung, drawn and quartered a few days later in London.

The Wintour Family of Huddington Court

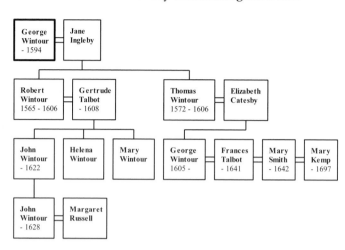

Were Robert and Thomas Wintour relatives of Rev. Fitzgerald Thomas Wintour? The line at Huddington Court died out and there is no proof, but the spelling of the surname and the class of people involved certainly tempts the supposition. Ultimately we may never know, but there must have been an important reason for the family to change the spelling of their surname and the latter is a possibility.

Having examined his forebears we can now return to Rev. Fitzgerald Thomas Wintour who we last met in the 1851 census returns. Ten years on we find him married, with four children and at work as the Rector of Hawerby in Lincolnshire:

1861 Census Return for Beesby Top, Hawerby.

Name	Age	Born	Occupation	Place of Birth
Fitzgerald Thomas Wintour	31	1829	Rector of Hawerby	Shudy Camps, Cambs.
Isabel M Wintour	28	1833		Thame, Yorks.
Mildred Wintour	3	1858	Scholar	London
Mary Wintour	3	1858		Hornsby, Lincs.
Isabel Wintour	2	1859		Hornsby
Fitzgerald Wintour	3mths	1861		Hornsby
Jane Smalley	29	1832	Housemaid	Horncastle, Lincs.
Ann Johnson	40	1821	Nurse	Yorkshire
Hannah Louise	27	1834	Cook	Leaton, Notts.
Sarah Smith	21	1840	Nursemaid	Little Hale, Lincs.

Fitzgerald Thomas Wintour married Isabel Milnes Gaskell in 1855 at Wakefield. Through Isabel's line of descent, the Fitzgerald Wintour's were descendants of Mary Tudor (1496-1533), the younger sister of King Henry VIII and Charles Brandon, Duke of Suffolk (c.1484-

1545) whom she married in 1515, through Mary Williams Wynn (1809-1869) who married James Milnes Gaskell of Yorkshire.

Isabel, born in 1835, was the daughter of James Milnes Gaskell and the above mentioned Mary Williams Wynn. We have already met James Milnes Gaskell when we examined his relationship with Anna Mildred Wintour, the Aunt of Thomas Fitzgerald Wintour. James was born in 1810 and was the only child of Benjamin and Mary Gaskell nee Brandreth of Thornes House near Wakefield. Benjamin had inherited Thornes House in 1805 from James Milnes, the MP for Maldon for whom it had been built in 1780. The grounds of Thornes House are now Thornes Park close to the city centre.

Benjamin was born in 1810 to Daniel Gaskell at Clifton Hall near Manchester. He was described as:

A quiet little man, very good natured, and simple almost as a child with very little conversation in him and much laudable desire of seeing everything that is to be seen and doing everything that is to be done to the last iota.

In 1806 he became MP for Maldon and began a long career in politics, a course that would be followed by his son.

James Milnes Gaskell

Educated at Eton College and Christ Church, Oxford, James left formal education, apparently, without attaining a degree. Whilst at Eton he met and became friends with William Ewart Gladstone. Gladstone (1809-1898) who went on to serve as Prime Minister on four separate occasions, first met his future wife, Catherine Glynne, at the London home of James Milnes Gaskell.

Whilst at Cambridge, James developed a fondness for the game of chess, playing Gladstone and others. He was present at the inaugural meeting of the Yorkshire Chess Association and was a member of the British Chess Associations chess congress of 1862. He was also recorded as playing chess in the context of the Houses of Parliament and attending St. George's Chess Club in London.

James became an MP for Wenlock in Shropshire from 1832 until his retirement in 1868. He served as Lord of the Treasury from 1841 to 1846 under Robert Peel's administration. In 1832 he married Mary Williams Wynn, the daughter of Charles Watkin Williams-Wynn who was also an MP. Their son, Charles George Milnes Gaskell (Isabel's younger brother) also followed a career in politics becoming an MP himself. James purchased the site of Wenlock Priory from his wife's cousin in 1857 and restored the ruins and developed the Priory Lodge into a family home. He died in London in 1873 aged 62 and was buried in the parish churchyard at Much Wenlock.

Charles George Milnes Gaskell attended Eton College and Trinity College, Cambridge. He became a Justice of the Peace, was Deputy Lieutenant for the West Riding of Yorkshire and Chairman of the West Riding County Council from 1893 to 1910. At the 1885 general election he was elected MP for Morley and retained the seat until he retired in 1892. He was made a Privy Councillor in 1908 and from 1902 to 1914 he was the Honorary Colonel of the 4th Battalion of the King's Own Yorkshire Light Infantry. He married Lady Catherine

Henrietta Wallop, daughter of the 5th Earl of Portsmouth in 1876. The couple lived at Thornes House and Wenlock Abbey. Lady Catherine was a minor author of the time who invited artistic and literary visitors to Wenlock which included Henry James and Thomas Hardy. Charles died in 1919 being survived by his wife, Lady Catherine, who died in 1935.

Cecil Grenville Milnes Gaskell was the eldest of James Milnes Gaskell's offspring and Isabel's older sister by only twelve months. Cecil (pronounced see-sul) married the critic and poet Francis Turner Palgrave (1824-1897) who was a lifelong friend of Alfred Lord Tennyson. Palgrave spent some time working in Whitehall before becoming Professor of Poetry at Oxford.

The Gaskell Family

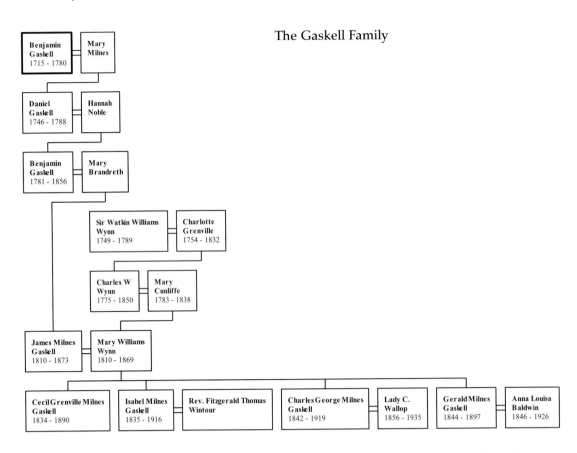

We have now examined the ancestry of both Fitzgerald Thomas Wintour and Isabel Milnes Gaskell. Both of their respective families were well connected, either with the older nobility, through the armed forces, politics or religion. We last caught up with them and their young family in 1851, by 1871, three years after their arrival in High Hoyland there had been a number of additions.

144

1871 Census Return for High Hoyland.

Name	Age	Born	Place of Birth
Fitzgerald T Wintour	41	1829	Cambridgeshire
Isabel M Wintour	36	1835	Yorkshire
Mildred Wintour	15	1856	London
Mary Wintour	13	1858	Lincolnshire
Isabel Wintour	12	1859	Lincolnshire
Evelyn Wintour	6	1865	Lincolnshire
Ann M Wintour	2	1869	Yorkshire
Kathleen Wintour	0	1871	Yorkshire
Zaiva Bovioni (Boarder)	22	1849	Italy
Ann Johnson (Servant)	49	1822	Yorkshire
Henriette Sechand (Servant)	19	1852	Swaziland
Mary Ann Lawson (Servant)	23	1848	Yorkshire
Harriet Johnson (Servant)	26	1845	Lincolnshire

We can see from this that the couple's eldest son, Fitzgerald was not at home, though he was only eleven years old. Additionally, a daughter, Violet had been born in 1866 but had died in infancy in 1869. The 1881 census return completes the family.

Name	Age	Born	Occupation	Place of Birth
Fitzgerald T Wintour	51	1829	Rector of High Hoyland	Gransden, Cambs.
Mary Wintour	23	1858		Hawerby
Francis Wintour	18	1863	Mechanical Engineering Apprentice	Hawerby
Anna Mabel Wintour	12	1869		High Hoyland
Charles J Wintour	9	1872	Scholar	High Hoyland
Margaret D Wintour	7	1874	Scholar	High Hoyland
Ulick F Wintour	3	1878		High Hoyland
Myra Lissamen	29	1852	Governess Teacher	Ansley, Yorks.
Ann Johnson	60	1821	Head Nurse	Altofts, Yorks.
Harriett Teale	68	1813	Cook	Newton, Yorks.
Sarah J Avnell	25	1856	Housemaid	Scarborough
Elizabeth Swift	20	1861	Kitchen Maid	Thornes
Ann E Binns	18	1863	Under Nurse	Normanton

Isabel was evidently away visiting relatives, though her absence was well covered due to the employment of six servants. Ulick was the last child born to Fitzgerald and Isabel, who, by the time of his birth was 43 years old. By 1891 only Mary, Isabel and Anna Mabel were still living at home, Ann Johnson, now aged 70, and still working as Head Nurse had passed the milestone of more than thirty years of service with the family.

Rev. Fitzgerald Thomas Wintour.   Isabel Wintour, pictured in 1880.

     A modern aerial view of the Rectory at High Hoyland.

The Rectory at High Hoyland, home to the Fitzgerald Wintour family.

The Rectory, High Hoyland, showing the garden terracing and steps.

The Rectory, High Hoyland.

With a family history like the Wintours' and Gaskells' one would expect the children of Fitzgerald and Isabel to pursue varied and sometimes dramatic careers and so is the case. We can now examine a little of their lives.

Major General Fitzgerald Wintour
Born in 1860 at Hawerby prior to his parents' removal to High Hoyland, Fitzgerald (known to family and friends as Gerald) entered the army in 1880. He served in Egypt in 1882 and Sudan between 1884-1886. He became a Captain of the Royal West Regiment in 1887 and served on the Northwest Frontier, India in 1897. Between 1899 and 1901 he fought in the Boer War in South Africa and perhaps as a result of his actions here was promoted the rank of Major in 1900. He became Lieutenant Colonel of the Norfolk Regiment in 1904 and Colonel in 1908. At the age of 54/55 he commanded a brigade in France between 1914-

1915 and rose to the rank of Major General. After 1915 he took on the role of Deputy Assistant Quarter Master General at the Headquarters of the Second Army. He retired in 1918 aged 58. During his time in India, Fitzgerald found time to play a first class cricket match. The averages for the 1892/3 season show that he played one match, made twelve runs in two innings, high score of nine and bowled one over taking one wicket for one run. He married Alice Vere Foster and had a son, Charles Vere Wintour. Fitzgerald died on 18 June 1949 at Broadstone, Dorset.

Charles Vere Wintour

Born in 1917 to Fitzgerald and Alice Vere Wintour, Charles attended Oundle School and Peterhouse University, Cambridge. Destined for a literary career he studied English and History and briefly edited Granta Magazine. Initially he took a job in advertising but left to join the Royal Norfolk Regiment in World War Two. His military action was notable and he was awarded the MBE, the Croix de Guerre and the Bronze Star. After the War, Charles became the lead writer for the Evening Standard and after a brief period with the Sunday Express returned as Deputy Editor. He became editor of the Daily Express in 1958 and then returned again to the Standard in 1959 as Editor, a post he remained in until 1976 when he left to become managing director of the Daily Express where he oversaw its transition from broadsheet to tabloid. In 1980 Charles joined the Press Council, serving for two years, he also launched the Sunday Express Magazine alongside his wife Audrey Slaughter, Working Woman magazine followed in 1984. In 1985 he became editor of the Press Gazette and gave advice upon the launch of new projects including Today, The Independent and TV-am. Charles retired in 1989 and spent his later years supporting the Liberal Democrats and chairing the regional National Art Collections Fund.

Anna Wintour

Born in 1949, Anna is the eldest daughter of Charles Vere Wintour and Eleanor Trego Baker. Educated at North London Collegiate School, Anna had a rebellious streak and developed an early interest in fashion. She became one of the first editorial assistants on Harper's & Queen magazine in 1970, though she made no secret that her ambition was to be the Editor of Vogue. By 1975 Anna was living and working in New York as a junior fashion editor. It was alleged that during this time she was introduced to Bob Marley, and disappeared with him for a week. A further position, as fashion editor for Viva magazine followed, though this ceased publication in 1978. Her ambition regarding Vogue magazine began to bear fruit by 1983 when she became its first creative director and by 1985 took over the editorship of the British version of the magazine. By 1988 she had achieved her dream and became editor of the American Vogue and oversaw three spin-off publications – Teen Vogue, Vogue Living and Men's Vogue during the first decade of the twenty-first century. Influential well outside the sphere of fashion, her salary was reported to be $2 million a year in 2005. Anna serves as a trustee of the Metropolitan Museum of Art in New York where she has organised benefits that have raised $50 million for the museum's

Costume Institute. She has also raised over $10 million for AIDS charities since 1990 and was awarded the OBE in the Queen's 2008 Birthday Honours list.

Captain Evelyn Fitzgerald Wintour

Evelyn chose the army for his career following in the footsteps of his elder brother. He became a Captain in the 3rd Madras Lancers. This regiment first came into being due to the East India Company in the late eighteenth century, changing its name to Lancers in 1891. By 1903 they had become the 28th Light Cavalry. In 1913 King George V approved the promotion of Evelyn from Major to Lieutenant Colonel. He died at his home, Shrubland's, Sunningdale, Berkshire in 1940.

Captain Charles John Wintour

Born in 1872, at High Hoyland, Charles John was nine years old and a scholar when the 1881 census was recorded. By 1891, now aged nineteen he had left Yorkshire for a life in the Royal Navy and can be found living in Portsmouth where he was recorded as a Midshipman. His career advanced, he was appointed to the Command of the Scout Cruiser *'Forward'* in 1911 and then promoted to Captain in June 1913. In December 1913 he was given the Command of the flotilla leader *'Swift'* and became the Captain of the Fourth Destroyer Flotilla. In 1915 he was appointed to the Command of the light cruiser *'Carysfort'*. The 1911 census returns record that Charles John was living at Medway near Gillingham and that he was, by now, married to Katherine Mary Keyes. The marriage actually took place in 1900 and produced a child, Rosemary.

By 1916 Charles John was in Command of a Faulknor class Destroyer called *'Tipperary'* which led the Fourth Destroyer Flotilla of the Grand Fleet commanded by Admiral Sir John Jellicoe. The Tipperary displaced 1610 tons and had a main armament of six 4-inch guns and a secondary armament of four 21-inch torpedo tubes. It could also make a top speed of 31 knots and had a normal crew of 197.

On 30th May 1916, intercepted German signals indicated that the German High Seas Fleet would be putting to sea to challenge the British control of the North Sea. Late on the 30th May the British Grand Fleet put to sea from its base at Scapa Flow in the Orkney Islands. Initial contact was made with the German High Seas Fleet off the coast of Jutland on the afternoon of the 31st May 1916.

At 12.03am on the night of 31 May/1 June Captain Wintour had become aware of a line of battleships closing through the darkness on his starboard side and converging on his course. To his port side lay the ships of the Royal Navy's 5th Battle Squadron. With the lead ship on his starboard quarter at a range of little more than 1100 yards a recognition signal was flashed out, which brought the immediate reply of powerful searchlights which illuminated the Tipperary. The battleships were the German ships *Westfalen,* trailed by *Nasau* and *Rheinland*. Between the battleships and the British 4th Destroyer Flotilla lay the German light cruisers "Stuttgart" and "Hamburg".

The German dreadnought SMS *Westfalen* of the German 1st Battle Squadron, 1st Division immediately opened fire on Tipperary with her secondary 5.9inch (15cm) armament. *Tipperary* was bombarded with 92 rounds of 5.9inch and 45 rounds of 3.5 inch shells, which reduced her to a blazing wreck within minutes, carrying away her bridge, including Captain Wintour and all upon it. A quote in a German observer wrote that:

> *The Tipperary put up a courageous fight, but the oil fuel caught fire and soon enveloped the ship in a fiery halo; charge after charge exploded in the ready ammunition racks near the guns, and shell after shell struck the ship forward, but the crew of the after gun continued to fire until the last man was killed.*

At 1.10am the German torpedo boats S53 and G88 encountered the burning wreck of the *Tipperary* and rescued eight crew from a raft in its proximity. At 3am the damaged German cruiser *Elbing* was scuttled by its crew, who then took to their ship's cutter. Nearby was the still burning, slowly sinking wreck of the *Tipperary,* and the cutter rescued the *Tipperary's* surgeon from the icy waters. She then encountered about a hundred of the destroyer's crew drifting partly in the water and partly on a life raft. They were unable to take any further survivors on, but burnt flares in the area with the hope, which proved in vain, of attracting British ships to their aid.

At approximately 2.00am HMS *Tipperary* finally sank and at approximately 5.00am four wounded survivors of HMS *Tipperary* were taken on board HMS *Sparrowhawk*. HMS *Sparrowhawk* had been in a collision and was no longer seaworthy. She was sunk at 8.00am after her crew and the survivors of *Tipperary* had been taken on board HMS *Marksman*.

Of the 197-crew members of HMS *Tipperary*, 185 had died (11 officers and 174 men) eight men were taken prisoner and four wounded men were saved by British forces. The Battle of Jutland had cost the Royal Navy three battle cruisers, three cruisers, eight destroyers, and 6,945 casualties. The Germans lost one battleship, one battle cruiser, four light cruisers, three destroyers, and 3,058 men.

In his report following the action, Admiral Sir John Jellicoe made the following mention of the loss of HMS *Tipperary:*

> *During the night the British heavy ships were not attacked, but the Fourth, Eleventh and Twelfth Flotillas, under Commodore Hawksley and Captains Charles J. Wintour and Anselan J. B. Stirling, delivered a series of very gallant and successful attacks on the enemy, causing him heavy losses. It was during these attacks that severe losses in the Fourth Flotilla occurred, including that of Tipperary with the gallant leader of the Flotilla, Captain Wintour. He had brought his flotilla to a high pitch of perfection, and although suffering severely from the fire of the enemy, a heavy toll of enemy vessels was taken, and many gallant actions were performed by the flotilla.*

Sir Ulick Fitzgerald Wintour

Born at High Hoyland in 1878, Ulick had a varied career as a civil servant. He can be found working for British Customs in May 1898, aged 20, in Shanghai, China. In 1910 he was appointed Commissioner General of the Silk Association and Silk Club and was Director of the British section in the Brussels exhibition that year. The London Gazette of 1918 records him receiving the honour of Officer of the Legion of Honour, it also states that he was a Parliamentary Secretary within the Ministry of Food and he was also the Director of Army Contracts between 1914 and 1917. The culmination of Ulick's career may have been with his involvement in the British Empire Exhibition in 1924.

The King had consented to be the Exhibition's patron, and was backed up by an Executive Council of 120 members. Ulick Fitzgerald Wintour was appointed General Manager and was described as a flamboyant personality whose plans for the Exhibition were grandiose in the extreme. He scornfully rejected the original proposal that it be held in the Crystal Palace. The Crystal Palace may have sufficed for Prince Albert, but in Wintour's schemes it ranked as little more than a hut. He envisaged a vast Imperial city in which every country in the Empire would have its own quarters and buildings. There would be extensive gardens, lakes, restaurants, dance halls and the biggest and best stadium on earth for spectacles and sporting events.

To find land for such a concept it was necessary to look beyond the boundaries of central London. Wembley, linked by Baker Street and Marylebone seemed ideal, and Wintour made an offer, which the owners accepted with alacrity, of £100,000 for 216 acres of farmland at Wembley Park.

By January, 1922 the funding target of £1 million had been reached, but it was clear that the Exhibition could not possibly be ready for its planned opening date in April, 1923. This was revised to April, 1924. Meanwhile, it was decided to concentrate upon building the stadium, which had been designed by Michael Ayrton and was to be constructed almost entirely of reinforced concrete.

In October there was a general election. The Liberals were defeated and the Conservatives returned for the first time since 1905. More significant, however, than the Tory victory, were the gains made by the Labour Party, which nearly doubled its strength to become the second largest party in the House. The new government was faced almost immediately with demands for an enquiry into the management of the Wembley Exhibition. There were criticisms of Wintour's cavalier behaviour and veiled hints of corruption in high places. As a result of a Board of Trade enquiry, Wintour was sacked, or, rather, bought off, and replaced by Sir James Stevenson, head of the Johnny Walker whisky firm.

King George V opened the Exhibition on St George's Day, 23 April 1924. The British Empire contained 58 countries at that time, and only Gambia and Gibraltar did not take part. It cost £12 million to stage and was the largest exhibition ever staged anywhere in the world, it attracted 27 million visitors.

Sir Ulick married Hylda Frances Catherine Garnett in 1901 (divorced 1923) who was a descendant of the Earls of Hastings and Margaret, Countess of Salisbury. He was invested as a Companion in the Order of St. Michael and St. George (CMG) and as a Companion in the Order of the Bath (CB). He left London in later life and retired to France, where he lived at Chemin des Mougins, Cap d'Antibes prior to his death at La Croix en Brie, Seine et Marne in 1947.

The Family of Rev. Thomas Fitzgerald Wintour – Rector of High Hoyland

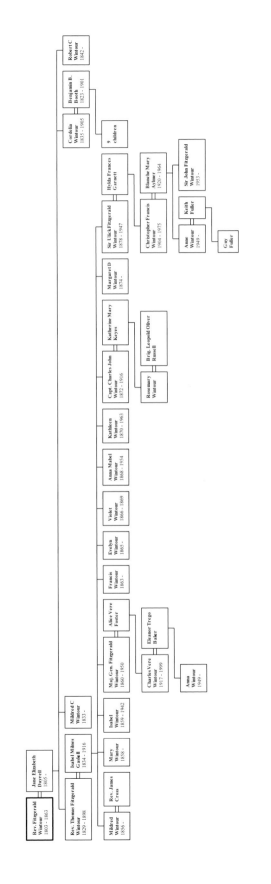

Rev. Fitzgerald Wintour 1803 - 1863
Jane Elizabeth Dayrell 1805 -

Rev. Thomas Fitzgerald Wintour 1829 - 1898
Isabel Milnes Gaskell 1834 - 1916
Mildred C Wintour 1833 -
Cordelia Wintour 1835 - 1905
Benjamin B. Booth 1823 - 1901
Robert C Wintour 1842 -

Rev. James Cross
Mildred Wintour 1856 -
Mary Wintour 1858 -
Isabel Wintour 1859 - 1942
Maj. Gen. Fitzgerald Wintour 1860 - 1950
Alice Vere Foster
Francis Wintour 1863 -
Evelyn Wintour 1865 -
Violet Wintour 1866 - 1869
Anna Mabel Wintour 1868 - 1954
Kathleen Wintour 1870 - 1963
Capt. Charles John Wintour 1872 - 1916
Katherine Mary Keyes
Margaret D Wintour 1874 -
Sir Ulick Fitzgerald Wintour 1878 - 1947
Hylda Frances Garnett

9 children

Charles Vere Wintour 1917 - 1999
Eleanor Trego Baker
Rosemary Wintour
Brig. Leopold Oliver Russell
Christopher Francis Wintour 1904 - 1975
Blanche Mary Aylmer 1920 - 1964

Anna Wintour 1949 -
Anne Wintour 1949 -
Keith Fuller
Sir John Fitzgerald Wintour 1953 -

Guy Fuller

Margaret (left) and Ulick Fitzgerald
Wintour photographed in 1881.

Mildred Wintour, photographed in 1862.

Wintour family group
dated 1865. Back row,
left to right: Mildred
Wintour, Isabel
Wintour (junior), Isabel
Wintour, Mary
Wintour. Seated on
Isabel's lap is Francis
(Frank) Wintour. Sat at
the front is Fitzgerald
(Gerald) Wintour, later
to become a Major
General in the Army.

Ulick Fitzgerald Wintour, with transport in the centre of High Hoyland, circa 1890's.

Isabel Wintour with the family dog, Teazle at Darton pond in September 1890.

Returning to the Rev. Fitzgerald Thomas, we must now examine the impact he made upon his appointment to the living of High Hoyland church.

High Hoyland village and its church had begun to decline in numbers due to changes brought about during the Industrial Revolution. Textile mills were established in Clayton West, which saw that village's population increase significantly. There was no Anglican Church in Clayton and so parishioners had to walk in all weathers to High Hoyland for services, baptisms, weddings and burials. Due to this absence a proliferation of non-conformist chapels had grown up in Clayton West which served the villagers' needs quite adequately and allegiance to the Anglican Church was largely over. In 1866, the absentee Rector of High Hoyland, Christopher Bird died and church life in the parish reached an all time low. Into this hostile environment stepped Fitzgerald Thomas Wintour.

Described as a young vigorous rector, he and his wife fully supported the authority and dignity of the Anglican Church. Fitzgerald Wintour fully understood the situation he found himself in and decided to discard the private pew system and to prepare for church life in Clayton West. Continual discord regarding the pews hampered his efforts and encouraged dissenters. Wintour planned to build a new church at Clayton West and in his first year in the Parish an old joiner's shop was rented for use as a Sunday school. The church was to be another matter. Most of central Clayton West was under the ownership of John Kaye, the wealthy owner of the woollen mills on Bilham Road. Wintour asked Kaye about a piece of land on Bilham Road for the proposed new church but Kaye refused as the congregation would have to pass the entrance to his home, The Park, thereby diluting his privacy. However, Kaye did suggest an alternative and in 1868 he conveyed to the Church Commissioners 780 square yards of the Well Yard. Outraged, the non-conformists united in opposition to the project and this coupled with various disputes with the builders led to the new church taking four years to complete, between 1871-1875. The foundation stone was laid by Lady Margaret Beaumont of Bretton Hall. The building committee included Walter Spencer Stanhope of Canon Hall and Thomas Norton of Bagden Hall. The church was consecrated in 1875 by the Bishop of Ripon, it had cost £2300 to erect. Fitzgerald Wintour expressed his opinion that the new edifice was too small, nor so magnificent as he would have had it but nevertheless it was sound and the best building in the village.

High Hoyland Girls' Club.

MANAGING COMMITTEE:

The Misses WINTOUR.   Mrs. APPLEYARD.

Miss CARR.   Mrs. DRAKE.

TREASURER:

Miss I. WINTOUR.

RULES.

1.—This Club is for Girls over 15, in the Parish of High Hoyland.

2.—Reading and Recreation Room to be open in the High Hoyland Reading Room during the winter months, every Monday evening, from 7 till 9.

3.—Members will pay 1d. a week (which will go towards defraying the expenses of the Club), and will receive a card of membership.

4.—Periodicals and Magazines will be supplied, also Games of various kinds.

5.—Materials for Plain and Fancy Work will be provided, for which members must pay before any article is taken home.

6.—Any member wishing to leave the Club, to give due notice and return their card of membership.

J. E. VENO, THE PRINTERY, BARNSLEY.

The High Hoyland Girls Club Rules, overseen by the ladies of the Wintour family.

The next step was to transfer the rights of High Hoyland Church to Clayton West. Wintour kept a register of attendance at High Hoyland, which revealed that the bulk of the worshippers came from Clayton West. He even noted that on certain days, including Good Friday there was frequently no congregation beyond that of his own family. The rector made the case that High Hoyland church was used for little other than burials and made a request to the Church Commissioners to close it. The church was in a state of dilapidation and the decision was agreed by an Order in Council in 1879. The closure was not without its dissenters, letters sent to the Barnsley Chronicle heavily criticised Wintour's decision. Indeed, they attacked some of his other moves including the appointment of young and inexperienced churchwardens around the year 1879. Lacking detailed knowledge about the situation their vitriol was misplaced. Wintour had, in fact, no choice but to appoint younger individuals since a more experienced householder who had been appointed was threatened by his employer and landlord with dismissal and eviction if he did not relinquish the role. The employer in this case was very likely to have been John Kaye, who had previously locked horns with Wintour over a typhoid epidemic in the village in 1874. Fitzgerald fought his corner and continued to press for change. His next project was to transfer the Rectory house to Clayton West, though he was also still open to restoring the old church at High Hoyland if the parish provided the money. Sunday afternoon services still took place here throughout the late nineteenth century, but the money was not forthcoming and so the church slowly began to decay.

Fitzgerald Thomas Wintour did not see the removal of the rectory as he died on 4 August 1898. He had been the Rector of High Hoyland/Clayton West for over 31 years and had overseen a revolution in Anglican worship in the parish. He was buried in what became the family tomb, in High Hoyland churchyard.

As plans were by now advanced for a new rectory to be built at Clayton West, Isabel Wintour bought the old one at High Hoyland. The census returns of 1901 record just Isabel and her daughter, Mary living here in a house that was once full of the life of the young Wintour family waiting to make a name for themselves in the world. The 1911 census returns record Isabel living at 8 Chester Terrace in London with the Jenkinson family, she died in 1916.

Fitzgerald and Isabel were recorded thus on the family grave:

Fitzgerald Thomas Wintour. For 31 years rector of this Parish. Born 12 April 1829. Died 4 August 1898. I am the resurrection and the life. Isabel Milnes Wintour. Born 27 July 1834. Died 17 June 1916. And now Lord what my hope - Truly my hope is even in thee.

Scissett

Porter's Lodge at the end of the 'Avenue' on Lower Clough House Lane.

The original end of Bagden Lane, at the point where it meets the footpath from Stoney Lane, circa 1900.

Gardens at Bagden Hall
prior to the First World
War.

Nortonthorpe Mill taken
from the bottom of
Highbridge Lane looking
down towards Cuttlehurst,
dated 1914.

159

The junction of the Wakefield and Barnsley Roads in the centre of Scissett. The mill chimney belonging to Beanland's can be seen to the extreme left.

Dearne Bridge with the end cottages of Dearne Terrace to the centre right. The millrace for Marshall Mill is in the foreground. Circa 1900.

Marshall Mill buildings photographed around 1900. The mill closed in 1919 and the final remaining buildings on the site were demolished in 1940.

Wakefield Road, Scissett, Morton's grocers and hardware shop is in the centre. Circa 1900.

Houses on Wakefield Road, on the left, just after where the more modern Pennine Way road turns off. The Scissett Working Men's Club was built just after the last terraced house on the right. Photograph dated 1907.

An aerial view of Skelmanthorpe Secondary Modern School, probably taken soon after it was built during the late 1940's.

Wakefield Road, Scissett. A village carnival passes by the site later to become the school playing fields. Circa 1920.

St. Augustine's church, built in 1839 and consecrated in 1840 and the War Memorial, circa 1920.

Busker Lane heading up towards Skelmanthorpe.

Busker Lane looking down the hill towards Scissett, circa 1920.

A view of Scissett from around half way up Busker Lane. Beanland's mill and chimney are prominent in the centre of the photograph.

Woodland Mount, Scissett.

Bradford & District Free Church Council meeting at Woodland Mount, Scissett, 18 July 1908.

Another scene of the Bradford & District Free Church Council meeting at Woodland Mount on 18 July 1908.

Taken just prior to the beginning of World War Two in 1939 and is the top class of Scissett Church of England school. Most of the pupils were among the first batch to enter Skelmanthorpe Secondary Modern when it opened in around 1947. Back row, left to right: C Tingay, M Douglas, B Robertshaw, A Bartlett, G White, K Dench, B Hunt, A Armitage, H Armitage, M Batty, F Exley, B Haigh, M Hepworth, J Ormondroyd, A Robinson, M Beever, M Firth, D Wilkinson, J Barraclough, F Fisher, B Tingay, M Smith, A Batty, G Dransfield. Seated: B Wilkinson, R White.

Scissett amateur dramatics in 1937 entitled 'Miss Hook of Holland'. It must be said that the actor playing the drunk has a gift for it.

Skelmanthorpe

Promotional postcard dating from around the 1930's.

Promotional postcard dating from around the 1930's.

Commercial Road, entering the Skelmanthorpe, circa 1900.

Commercial Road, entering Skelmanthorpe in 1928.

Free Church School Feast on land that later became the triangle in July 1906.

Top of Town, prior to the triangle being made in 1919. The photo dates to around 1900.

Temperance demonstration on Commercial Road in 1910.

Considered to be the oldest part of Skelmanthorpe, these buildings occupy a site known as Gill Gate. Prior to their being built Gill Gate consisted of much older cottages and farms but these were demolished around the 1880's. The Star Public House may also have formed a part of this older site. New Street can be seen heading away on the left, the Liberal Club can also be seen in the centre, the photograph dates from the early twentieth century.

Taylor & Fields off licence and grocers can be seen to the right on Commercial Road. To the left of their premises is the Liberal Club, built in 1911.

Commercial Road, circa 1930's. The Working Men's Club is the nearest building on the right.

Commercial Road, circa 1900. Buckley's confectionery shop can be seen to the left whilst to the right is the entrance to the former Wesleyan Chapel.

This scene is a reverse of the previous photograph, again taken around 1900, the entrance to the former Wesleyan Chapel is to the left on Commercial Road, looking towards the direction of Huddersfield.

Commercial Road, 1928. The entrance to New Lane is on the left.

Commercial Road, circa 1928. The entrance to Pilling House (built by Edwin Field) is to the left.

The Windmill Inn and cottages circa 1890's. The end house on the terraced row to the left was demolished during the early 1930's.

Highbridge Lane, Skelmanthorpe, around the 1930's.

HIGHBRIDGE LANE, SKELMANTHORPE.

Highbridge Lane in 1939. The cemetery chapel, built in 1885, can be seen to the right.

Coal treatment works at Park Gate around 1900. This was the reception area for coal mined at Emley to be screened and washed before being despatched around the country by train.

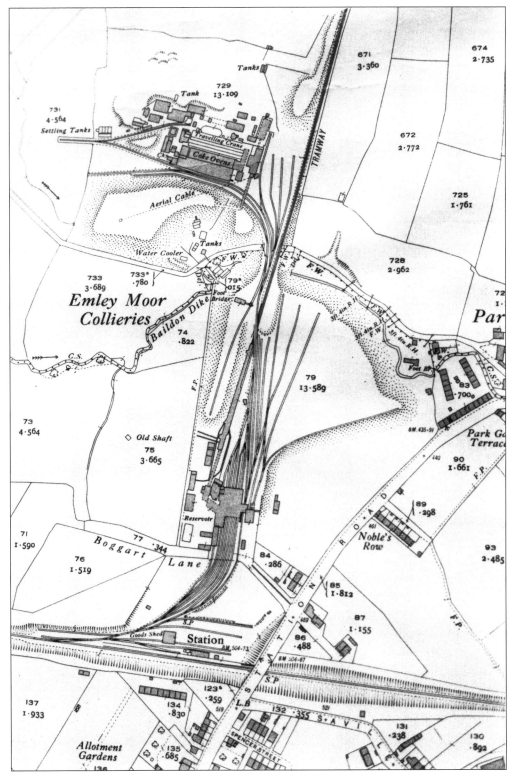

Map showing the Emley Moor Collieries, the station at Skelmanthorpe and the area between Boggart Lane and the railway line where the buildings in the previous photograph were later to be erected.

The Mount, on Station Road, built by the Field family in the mid nineteenth century.

Station Terrace, circa 1900.

Score Hill on Saville Road, early twentieth century.

Top of Score Hill. The buildings to the right, were built by the Jepson family as housing for employees who worked in their small textile mill. Circa 1900.

Dale Bottom, Elm Street. The entrance to Gibb Lane can be seen splitting the rows of terraced cottages. Circa 1900.

Elm Street, early twentieth century.

ELM ST SKELMANTHORPE

The Old Globe Hotel at the top of Elm Street, early twentieth century.

Longroyds Lodge, once the residence of staff employed by textile mill owner, John Thomas Field at the entrance to his property. Circa 1890.

Longroyd Lodge, with the main house in the background, taken in around 1900. Note the old farm cultivator laying the field in the foreground.

Parkgate Farm behind the bridge over Park Gate Dyke. Early twentieth century.

Greenside around 1900. The coalbunker to the left served a single storey property, which consisted of just two rooms, a living room and a handloom weaving room.

Pilling House, built by Edwin Field, pictured around 1930.

Father and son dwellings. To the left is Pilling House built by Edwin Field to the right is Longroyds built by John Thomas Field. Circa 1930.

Skelmanthorpe.

Longroyds, built by John Thomas Field (1866-1938).

St. Aidan's parish church, with the vicarage to the left, circa 1930.

The National school destroyed by fire on 17 November 1909. Re-building was undertaken and the school re-opened on 12 December 1910.

Interior of the school after the disastrous fire of 1909.

FONT SKELMANTHORPE CHURCH

The font at St. Aidan's church. This font is believed to date from before 1100 and originally resided in High Hoyland church.

Interior of St. Aidan's church, around the early twentieth century.

Primitive Methodist Chapel on Pilling Lane. Originally built in 1836 and extended in 1864. The extension can clearly be seen, half way down the side of the chapel, in this photograph dating circa 1910.

Primitive Methodist Chapel group, taken in 1880, in front of the chapel.

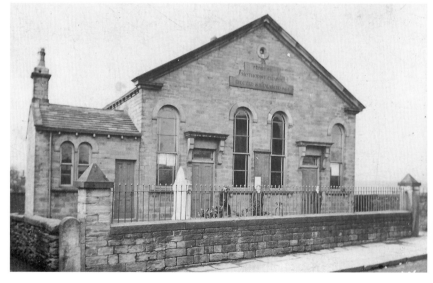

Primitive Methodist chapel on Pilling Lane.

Zion Wesleyan Reform chapel, built in 1854 and enlarged in 1865 pictured prior to World War One.

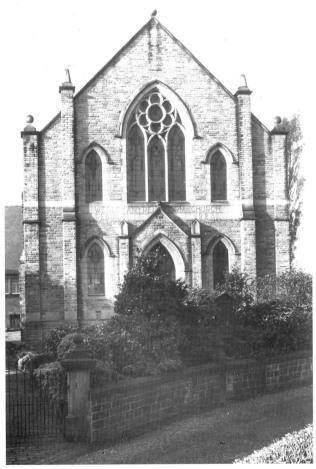

The new Zion Wesleyan Reform chapel, on Gibb Lane, after complete demolition of the old building. The first stone of the new chapel was laid on 22 September 1923.

STONE-LAYING CEREMONY
NEW SUNDAY SCHOOL
WES' REFORM CH SKELMANTHORPE
JULY 26-1913

Stone laying ceremony for the new Sunday school at the Zion Wesleyan Reform chapel dated 26 July 1913.

Zion Wesleyan Reform Sunday school and chapel, circa 1920. The last service held at the chapel took place in April 2012; the last christening took place on 8 April when ten-month-old Stanley Simpson-Lockwood was baptised. Dwindling congregations saw the reluctant closure of the chapel. Its last full-time minister gave his final sermon around thirty years before the closure but services continued with a rotation of mainly local preachers. During the early 1990's the upper level of the building was removed as the congregation had shrunk but by 2012 only around ten people were attending services. The last event held at the chapel was a coffee morning for the charity Christian Aid on 19 May 2012.

Interior of the Primitive Methodist chapel in 1903. The choir includes: Harry Lawton, Willie Radley, Mrs Derbyshire, Ethel Ruth Shaw, Alfred Shaw and Annie Senior.

Primitive Methodist group, taken at the front of the chapel, circa 1903.

Skelmanthorpe Council school pupils taken around the late 1890's.

Skelmanthorpe Council school pupils taken around 1900.

Primitive Methodist Boys and Girls Endeavour Classes around 1924. Back row, left to right: Phyllis Radley, Ada Firth, Isabel Radley, Alice Haigh, Cissie Lodge, Doreen Spencer, Evelyn Vera Marsden, Annie Kaye. Middle row, left to right: Annie Ellis, Alice Lawton, Harriet Lawton, Louie Radley, Mabel Hurn, Muriel Swallow, Lilly Firth, Francis Haigh, Kathleen Peel, Bessie Radley, Hilda Lockwood, Mabel Wilson. Front row, left to right: Sam Ellis, Cyril Lockwood, Stanley Haigh, Eric Turton, Ralph Collier, Jonas Lawton, Alwyn Wadsworth, George Henry Booth, William Dobson, Tom Wainwright.

Primitive Methodist Scripture Examination Shield Winners, circa 1950's. The back row includes: Mrs J H Fisher, Rosalie Fenton, Margaret Mathers, Cecil Cockshaw, Russell Waddington, Annie Senior, Jean Stephenson, Joan Stringer, Brian Buckenden, David Harris. The front row includes: Mavis Asquith, Dorothea Stringer, Mildred Armitage, Jean Harris, Joan Lawton, Geoffrey Firth, David Waddington, Alfred Kettle, John Senior.

Primitive Methodist chapel school feast 1909.

Skelmanthorpe Football Club, circa 1910.

Skelmanthorpe Football Club Juniors in 1908/9. George Henry Ellis is second from the left on the front row.

Skelmanthorpe Football Club 1938/9 season. Top: H Carter, Second row: E Armitage, L Turner. Third row: A Lawton, S Thornton, Sel Turton. Fourth row: D Ferguson, S Rangely, J Fisher, J Law, B Greaves, T Redgewick, C Dalton, H Senior, A Hirst, S Turton, T Lodge, K Haigh, E Law, J Broadbent. Fifth row: D Burkinshaw, H Bowden, H Dearnley, E Fisher, H Spring. Front: D Lodge.

Taken at the same time as the previous photograph, this one dispenses with managers, trainers and other officials and only includes the actual players from 1938/9.

Skelmanthorpe cricket team dating to 1908. George Wainwright is the umpire on the far left in the long white coat. The cricket team had its origins in the 1870's and by 1880 were playing matches at the rear end of the Co. Op. Farm. The current club was founded in 1892 and in 1900 moved to the present club location on Lidgett Lane.

Liberal Club billiard team, circa 1920's. Tommy Spring is second from the right on the back row. Fred Biltcliffe is second from the left on the front row.

Skelmanthorpe tennis enthusiasts, probably during the 1930's. Back row, left to right: Henry Hubert Lawton, Clifford Stephenson, Gilbert Collier. Second row: Ivy Collier, Edith Mathews, unknown, Elsie Radley, Miriam Ellis, ? Tunnecliffe, Mary Lizzie Lawton. Third row: Nellie Lodge, Alice May Appleyard, Mrs Reverend Laughton, Melinda Woodhead, Annie Turton.

Skelmanthorpe Primitive Methodist Chapel put on the operetta *Snow White* in 1919. The cast were, back row, left to right: Alice Ann Beevers, Alice Lodge, Rhoda Firth, Cessie Lodge, Leonora Pearson, Ada Firth, Lena Pearson. Second row: Bertha Lodge, Ivy Lawton, May Lodge, Edna Lodge, Harry Shaw, Miriam Ellis, Herbert Haigh (pianist), Gladys Radley, Alice Radley, Annie Turton. Third row: Hilda Radley, Walter Holmes, Percy Dyson, Florence Lodge, Polly Dyson, Stanley Haigh, Walter Dyson, Leslie Turton, Olive Roberts, Alice Dyson. Fourth row: Rhoda Smith, Louise Radley, Irene Hey, Lily Firth, Mary Swift, Elsie May Booth, Miriam Derbyshire, Irene Firth, Mary Lodge, Clara Lydall, Doreen Spencer. Front row: Rene Morley, Eddie Morley, Tom Wainwright, Donald Holmes, Sam Lodge, Cyril Lockwood, Edwin Dyson.

Primitive Methodist Chapel, younger members of the congregation and choir in 1935.

Primitive Methodist cast for an unknown production, circa 1919.

Primitive Methodist actors in a 1955/6 Sunday school pantomime of *Mother Goose*.

Primitive Methodist players in *Mother Goose*, 1955/6.

Primitive Methodist Sunday school pantomime *Babes in the Wood* 1959/60.

Primitive Methodist players, circa 1960.

Primitive Methodist female performers, circa 1960's.

A 'sand dance' being performed by two of the Primitive Methodist Chapel actresses, circa 1960's.

David Carter (seated) and Harry Fisher, the Skelmanthorpe Open Air Singing Band.

Albert Shakesby, a travelling Evangelist who visited Skelmanthorpe. Shakesby (1873-1949) was born and lived in Hull. He became a small time criminal, mainly fighting and theft. He also became a boxer and weightlifter and worked in music halls. After experiencing a vision in a chapel in 1904 he completely mended his ways and became a convert, eventually preaching far and wide.

202

Mr West of Denby Dale, he was a local lay preacher on the Clayton West chapel circuit.

Fieldhouse Moorhouse, a well known local character who was heavily involved with the Primitive Methodist chapel and a local lay preacher. He was born in 1856 and married Elizabeth Tyas in 1880.

The travelling barrel organ visits Skelmanthorpe. Known in the village as the 'jingleairy man' he was a well-known visitor though in the photograph a young girl is taking the money rather than the monkey he usually brought with him.

Clarence Bradbury, the self styled 'Mayor of Skelmanthorpe' in front of his house on Commercial Road, at the bottom of Pickles Lane. It is currently unknown as to why he is holding the fox.

Skelmanthorpe children as Red Cross Nurses, 19 September 1914. Taken only a short while after Britain had declared war on Germany on 4 August.

SKELMANTHORPE CHILDREN AS RED CROSS NURSES SEPT. 19 1914

Road repairs in Skelmanthorpe during the 1950's. Heating and planing the old surface before a new topcoat was spread over it.

Skelmanthorpe station, circa 1960's.

"SCOUTS" BONFIRE
"JUBILEE"
SKELMANTHORPE.

Skelmanthorpe Scouts bonfire to celebrate the Silver Jubilee of King George V in 1935. The bonfire was built in the former feast field at the bottom of Barrow Stead.

Primitive Methodist float, taken during the 125th celebrations of the foundation of the chapel in 1961.

AS THEY MET IN BLACKER WOOD
BEFORE CHURCH WAS BUILT IN 1836

Primitive Methodist float, taken near the triangle, during the 125th Commemoration celebrations in 1961.

Some of the staff employed at Edwin Field's Tentercroft Mill probably during the 1930's.

This photograph is thought to perhaps be some of the staff employed at Edwin Field's Tentercroft Mill around 1932.

Office staff employed at Tentercroft Mill during the First World War. The photograph is dated 20 March 1916.

Warehouse staff employed at Edwin Field's in 1914. Back row, left to right: Norman Appleyard, Arthur Lawton, Fred Hobson, Vincent Firth, Jack Dyson, Albert Wragg. Middle row: George Ferguson, Ralph Greaves, Arthur Barraclough, Herbert Gray, Edgar Armitage. Front row: Bob Billcliffe, Joseph Clegg.

Skelmanthorpe Co. Op. staff with the Manager, A Turner seated in the middle. Mr Turner was the manager between 1903 and 1918. The photograph was taken in front of the garage door in what is now the present day car park.

Skelmanthorpe Co. Op. Centenary Committee 1934. Taken in front of the building used as a slaughterhouse in what is now the present day car park.

The staff of Field & Bottrill's who formed a male voice choir in order to take on their rivals at Edwin Field's to decide who was best. The winners were men of Field & Bottrill. Largely as a result of this village competition the Skelmanthorpe Male Voice Choir was formed. The photograph is taken in front of the finishing department.

86. The World War Two district wardens, Post 89.12 Skelmanthorpe. Seated fourth from the left is Norman Stead, the Head Warden in Skelmanthorpe. To his left is William Herbert Senior, who became a very notable and well-respected local historian.

Skelmanthorpe Wesley Guild line up for a group photograph on an outing to Gunthwaite on Whit-Monday 1910.

Band of Hope Temperance demonstration, prior to setting off at the back of the Wesleyan chapel in 1907.

Probably employees at the Park Gate site of Emley colliery, circa 1900.

Band of Hope outing to Endcliffe Woods, May 1918. Endcliffe Woods are to the South West of Sheffield and are a part of Endcliffe Park, created in 1887 for Queen Victoria's Golden Jubilee in 1887.

Skelmanthorpe Wesleyan chapel ladies, during the early twentieth century.

The Skelmanthorpe Wesleyan Reform choir pictured by the chapel doors in 1909.

An early twentieth century Wesleyan chapel choir.

Centenary Camp Meeting 15 May 1907. The photograph is taken between Lodge Street and Queen Street.

The visit of the President of the Primitive Methodist Sunday school in March 1986. Former MP Ann Taylor is in the centre of the photograph, at the far right is local historian, the late Tom Wainwright.

Fancy dress competitors in Skelmanthorpe taking part in celebrations to mark the Coronation of King George VI on 12 May 1937. The caption under the photograph reads 'The Wise Men from the East'.

Selected Historical Notes

Extract from the *Huddersfield Examiner* **dated 1934.**
Skelmanthorpe: How Times Have Changed - Old Feast Days Recalled - Quaint Village with a Bracing Air.

As I left Skelmanthorpe I thought to myself, this is, above all, a true Yorkshire village. Believe me, last impressions in this world are far more important and enduring than first impressions, whatever may be said to the contrary. My first judgement was as worthless as it was unfavourable. It was not even interesting.

But after I had been there three hours, I began to see why many of the villagers have lived there thirty, forty or sixty years. Another three hours and I might have become one of them myself.

The reason is, of course, that the village and its people are one, ideally combined. In the course of two or three centuries they have grown into each other so much that today disintegration is unthinkable. I have not a doubt that the same family names will be current a hundred years hence.

When I arrived at Skelmanthorpe (which lies by the way, between Shelley and Clayton West, and has a population of about three thousand) I spun a coin to decide (as one might do in every village) which fount of village wisdom I should visit first. It fell tails so I strolled into the public house. An oldish, philosophical looking man was draining a glass of bitter and in just the time that it takes a young man to dispose of half a pint and an oldish man to dispose of a whole one, he was moving gingerly to the doorway, having consented to be my guide.

Sunlight flooded the street as we stepped out of the dark. Skelmanthorpe's main street, though it holds the Council building and a chapel, is not 'true Skelmanthorpe' but rather nothing more than a bypass for transient motorists. It is in the little streets on either side that the quaintest and prettiest buildings are to be seen. Accordingly, after proceeding a few paces and pausing to glance at a motor-car which, to the intense delight of a cluster of villagers, had been playing battering ram with a wall, we turned down a lane to the left and came almost immediately into view of one of the most picturesque old houses I have seen for some time – a house dating from the seventeenth century.

As we went further, my guide pointed out to me in the distance a colliery which draws two or three hundred of its workers from Skelmanthorpe, though it is not working more than three days a week. My guide pointed out also the Skelmanthorpe Co-Operative Society, which he proudly told me, was the oldest registered Co-Operative Society in the country. It was started a hundred years ago this year and registered in 1834. In Saville Street is what must be the queerest hobby in all Skelmanthorpe. Mr Albert Lambert, a scrap iron dealer, indulges in it. He has a rockery about fifteen yards long, which he bedecks with all the mantelpiece ornaments he can come across – china dogs, little statues and other knick-knacks. Most of them he obtains from local tip heaps, but his hobby is well known in the locality that when of the kind are no longer wanted they are often brought to him direct. He has been collecting for four years. Unfortunately, the urchins of Skelmanthorpe regard his array as fair game for their prowess with stones, and as there is no protection between it and the street, damage is often being done.

The feast is the biggest event of the year at Skelmanthorpe. It is not, luckily, the riotous affair it was a century and a half ago, but it has preserved a lot of its character. Towards the end of the eighteenth century, bull-baiting, bear-baiting and organised dog-fighting were among the amusements, the whole being accompanied by as many drunken brawls as could be fitted in during the week in which the feast was in progress.

Skelmanthorpe church, which struck our eyes as we re-entered the main street is an undistinguished but serviceable building, the foundation stone of which was laid in 1894. It was to have had a tower, but sufficient money was never forthcoming.

I sought out Mr Fred Lawton of Bentley House, who knows perhaps as much about the village as anyone. Mr Lawton is seventy-six years old. Seventy years ago in the bad old days of child labour, he first went to work in a mill. I had heard that Skelmanthorpe was once famous for it's 'poising'– that is kicking bouts. None of that, Mr Lawton told me takes place now. And the 'biting' for which Skelmanthorpe was once renowned is now but a tradition. Today the village is the best behaved in the country. Biting, in the old days, it is said, was a Skelmanthorpe man's own peculiar way of settling an argument. In America they 'fill you with lead'. In most places in England you give (or receive) a 'sock in the jaw'. In Skelmanthorpe, if you annoyed them, they bit you, savagely in the ear. It may sound incredible, but I am told that it is only a few years since that a man was still living in the village who had been deprived of one of his ears in this way.

I had still made no acquaintance with two features of the life of the village, and I wanted to learn something about them before I left. I wanted to have a look at some of the handlooms and see something of the canary breeding. The passing of the handloom in Skelmanthorpe is not a matter of sentiment only. It means tragedy. Depression in the wool trade of recent years has been such that although there are a dozen or two of these Heath-Robinson like machines still in existence – out of dozens and dozens which once brought a comfortable living to those who owned and worked them – there is not now, I am informed by those who should know, one single hand-loom in use. As the months pass, dust settles thickly upon them, the intricate cord and woodwork begins to collapse and their owners, seeing no prospect of any weaving ever coming to them again, let them literally fall to pieces. It is the only trade many of the people know. You can tell at a glance a cottage which has a handloom upstairs. I visited two or three such cottages and saw the looms (or what remained of them) in the bedrooms.

But if there is despair in the hearts of the weavers, the canary fanciers have reason to twitter as joyfully as the golden proteges. Canaries are selling as well as ever. One cottage

I went into had stacks and stacks of cages. The birds are worth anything up to £1 a pair, and exceptional specimens much more, of course. Some of the birds have been exported as far afield as America and the local fanciers have taken many prizes at the Crystal Palace and other big shows. There is also a Skelmanthorpe show each year. Extraordinary care is taken with the birds and the owners are extremely proud of them.

In the evening, rather tired, but certainly interested, I sought out the Vicar of Skelmanthorpe to hear a final judgement on the village. The vicarage stands aloof from most of the village, like a guardian angel, keeping a kind but firm watch. The Rev. E Teale, the vicar, surprised me by putting into words what I had been thinking all the time: Skelmanthorpe is so bracing.

> *"It has the best climate of any village I know, principally because of this I have refused several offers during the past ten years of other livings".*

And Mr Teale ought to know a good climate when he gets one. He has lived in the Canadian Rockies. Over a cup of tea, Mr Teale discussed village life with me. I learnt that Skelmanthorpe takes a fairly keen interest in politics; that the days of foolish thrift among the villagers – when money was hoarded in stockings – have vanished; and that most of them would be quite content not to stir from their native green during the rest of their lives – which by now did not surprise me.

When I left Skelmanthorpe the sun was low and the villagers, as is their practice were clustering in groups along t'top, exchanging the gossip of their simple but idyllic lives. I left with real regret. There is only one thing I cannot understand. Why have they allowed so charming a man as Mr Teale to remain a bachelor?

The Rev. Edwin Teale MC – Vicar of Skelmanthorpe 1919-1945.

Born in 1892, Edwin Teale was destined for a career in religion from an early age. He was confirmed in 1895, aged 13 by his late sponsor, Sidney M Smith, the Vicar of Hebden Bridge. Prior to taking Holy Orders, Edwin entered Cambridge at Easter 1900, reading divinity. He graduated with a BA (Hon) in 1903. He then spent much of the next two years attending the Theological College at Ordsall Hall, Salford. He was ordained as a Deacon in June 1905, at Manchester Cathedral at the age of 23 and in June 1906 was ordained a Priest during which time he had taken up the position of Curate at St. Mathews, Little Lever, near Bolton. He left this position in 1908, when he returned to Hebden Bridge where he remained as a Curate until 1911.

At this point he answered an appeal made by the Archbishop's Mission to Western Canada Fund, to minister to the rapidly growing number of new Anglicans settled in the region. The first party, to Edmonton, under the Mission Head, Reverend William Grenville Boyd (Chaplain to the Archbishop of Canterbury) included a handful of clergy and left England in April 1911. Edwin was one of the handful. His first post was to the Lytton Indian Mission in British Columbia, between 1911 and 1912. Lytton was on the Caribou Gold Rush Trail and was a stopping place for prospectors to replenish supplies and to rest.

A tiny place, its population in 2010 was only 330. It is possible Edwin was actually based at the Mission House at Edmonton, this was the base from where the clergy were despatched to their various undertakings. Between 1912 and 1914 Edwin ministered at the Church of St. Aidan & St. Hilda, Rexboro, which was about fifty miles West of Edmonton.

At the outbreak of the First World War Edwin returned to England as soon as possible. Four days after his arrival he had enlisted in the Territorial Reserve, taking a commission in the Army Chaplains Department. He served at Gallipoli between June 1915 and January 1916 with the Mediterranean Expeditionary Force and was mentioned in despatches as being wounded in July 1916. He was then posted to Mesopotamia to the Tigris Corps where he was promoted to Temporary Chaplain, 3rd Class (the equivalent of a Major) in December 1916 and where he remained for the duration of the conflict. During this time he was awarded the Military Cross. Family tradition holds that Edwin received the medal for bravery under enemy fire as he rescued a wounded fellow officer in the Gallipoli campaign, but official documents

The Rev. Edwin Teale - 1892-1953.

clearly state the action took place in Mesopotamia. The Tigris Corps were engaged in trying to raise the Siege of Kut-al-Amara where imperial forces had been trapped during a retreat from Baghdad but despite initial success the Turks held out and the garrison at Kut surrendered in 1916. Action resumed later in the year and Kut finally fell in February 1917 and the Tigris Corps were the first British into Baghdad on 11 March 1917. From this point onwards they became an army of occupation, consolidating the city and surrounding area. Edwin remained with the Division until it was disbanded in 1919.

After the war Edwin returned to Yorkshire, to Skelmanthorpe to become its new Vicar. Originally he rode to Skelmanthorpe from his home in Bradford but after a nasty crash and time spent in hospital he moved to the village and settled at the vicarage. Here he was cared for by Tom Lumbley Hampshire (gardener) and his wife, Mary Ellen nee Heath (housekeeper) who stayed with him up until his retirement. He kept in touch with his old war comrades; indeed his former batman would stay with him for four days every year. Two local mill owners, Herbert Selwyn Jackson (Greenside Mill) and Major Claude Rigby (Elm Mill), both formerly of the West Riding Regiment would join him to attend race meetings in Doncaster and elsewhere.

Described as a quiet man but sociable in his own way, kindly, amiable, highly educated and able to talk about any subject, Edwin did not reveal to anyone his experiences of the war. He organised outings, croquet on the Vicarage lawn and was President of the Skelmanthorpe Male Voice Choir in 1934. He was also a Chairman of the Urban District Council. In 1945, Edwin retired to Llandudno. He died aged 71 on 27 June 1953.

Upon leaving Skelmanthorpe Edwin wrote an open letter in the Parish Magazine:

By the time you have received this magazine I shall have left Skelmanthorpe. It has been my home for 26 years. In this village which I have grown to love, I have attempted to make known to you the Gospel of Jesus Christ. During all those years I have felt I lived among friends who were always glad to receive me into their houses, and I have been very happy indeed. I leave with the very deepest regret, but I shall carry with me very pleasant and happy memories which, I am sure, the years will not fade.

Upper Denby * Ingbirchworth * Birdsedge

An unknown group of children all set for a donkey ride, on Bank Lane at the entrance to Manor Farm. Dated to around 1910.

Arthur Heath astride the family horse, used for fetching stock for the grocers shop on Smithy Hill. Pictured on Smithy Hill at the entrance to Back Lane around 1900.

The Upper Denby joiner and undertaker, Joe Willie Heath, with his son, Harry, pictured on Smithy Hill with, now demolished, coal bunker and cottages to the left. To the right are the buildings that used to occupy the village green. In the background are the cottages on Milnes Row and Denby Lane. Circa 1920.

Locals gather for a photo opportunity outside the New Inn on Denby Lane, prior to the First World War.

Gunthwaite Spa, a scene little changed today, though the warning notice about trespassing is long gone.

The bye-wash at Ingbirchworth Reservoir, showing the 65.6 foot high dam, taken around 1908.

Pupils at Birdsedge village school taken in 1908/9.

The Council School at Birdsedge.

An unknown woman poses for a photograph with her pet bulldog in Birdsedge, just off the Penistone Road. Birdsedge farm can be seen to the top right. Circa 1940.

The High Flatts tug-of-war team in 1909. It is imagined that the serious looking men's eight had been victorious as they stand with a grand looking clock. It should be remembered that the tug-of-war was an Olympic sport from 1900 to 1920 and so was taken very seriously.

Selected Historical Notes

The Rectors of Upper Denby

In Denby & District IV, I examined the lives of the clergy of Upper Denby. I noted in the clergy listing on page 77 that Joseph Horsfall was the Perpetual Curate till at least 1819. In fact he remained in this position until his death in 1820 upon which the Assistant Curate, Brice Bronwin was made Perpetual Curate, his patron being Martin Joseph Naylor – Vicar of Penistone. Bronwin had been Assistant Curate since 11 August 1816 on a stipend of £55 plus surplice fees, his patron then having been Joseph Horsfall. I suggested that Bronwin's Perpetual Curacy had begun earlier than the recorded 1830 and this has now been proved. This means that the name John Brownhill recorded as being a Curate at Upper Denby in 1822 can now, at last, be removed from the list entirely.

Rev. Job Johnson

In Denby & District IV, I examined the lives of the Ministers of Upper Denby Church. The story of one individual had an unsatisfactory ending as he moved away from the village before he died. I had evidence that he had made the short move to Huddersfield and this has in fact proved to be correct. Rev. Job Johnson died on 1 December 1891 whilst residing at 22 West Hill, Huddersfield, aged 75. His death was noted in the village as reported in the *Huddersfield Examiner* dated 12 December 1891.

Denby Conservative Club – Presentation

On Friday night, last week, the members of the Denby Conservative Club and other friends assembled in the club-room to present to Mr C Hargreaves a handsome marble timepiece as a mark of esteem and a token of appreciation of services rendered during the past fourteen years as Secretary of the Club.

At the conclusion of the presentation, that Gentleman (Charles Hargreaves) rose, and, addressing the members of the Conservative Club said they all heard with great and deep sorrow that their old former Vicar, Mr Johnson had, that day, been buried at Boston Spa. All in Denby and surrounding district highly respected and loved the old Vicar, and if he could have been interred at Denby, there would have been a host of friends gathered around his grave. All present knew the benevolence and kind-heartedness of the departed one, and of Mrs Johnson, likewise; and therefore, he need say nothing more on those points, but would propose:

That the Secretary of the Conservative Club be authorised to write a letter of condolence to the family of the late Rev. J Johnson and to assure them that had it not been for the distance to Boston Spa, many would have been there to pay a last token of respect to him.

Mr Arthur Priest seconded the proposition and suggested that some memorial to Mr Johnson should be erected in Denby Churchyard by the parishioners. Mr Arthur Kenyon supported the resolution, saying he had a profound respect for their late Vicar, who, he had hoped, might have ended his days in Denby. Mrs Johnson was an indefatigable worker in temperance and church work, and he could inform them that a wreath had been sent to Mr Johnson's funeral from himself and Denby friends, and he thought they could place some memorial at the East end of the Churchyard, where some members of Mr Johnson's family were buried. Mr J Micklethwaite gave an account of the labours of the late Vicar and of his unbounded liberality and goodness of heart, lamenting that he had ever left Denby and that without claiming a part of the living. He wished there were more clergy like Mr Johnson. The proposition was carried, after a few remarks on the coincidence of the presentation to Mr Hargreaves and now having the melancholy duty of raising one to the memory of one of the best men who ever lived in Denby, and whom all respected while living, and mourned for when gone. Mr Ernest T Moore and Mr Arthur Kenyon were authorised to get some bills printed, calling a public meeting to consider the desirability of erecting some memorial to the memory of the late Rev. Job Johnson.

Rev. Johnson had spent his last two years in Huddersfield living alone. His wife, Mary Anne had died on 31 August 1889 and been taken to Boston Spa for burial. This was the reason that the good Reverend was not buried at Denby, or even in Yorkshire, as he wished to be close to his wife after death.

On her gravestone Mary Anne was noted to be the wife of Rev. J Johnson – Sometime Vicar of Denby. A short inscription on the stone reads:

She is not dead but only lieth sleeping,
In the safe refuge of her Masters breast,
And far away from sorrow, toil and weeping,
She is not dead but only taking rest.

Her husband would undoubtedly, have chosen the words upon the gravestone.

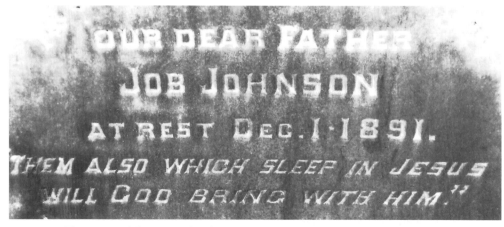

The grave of the Rev. Job Johnson. The inscription is carved on the reverse side of his wife's gravestone in Boston Spa.

The gravestone of Mary Ann Johnson in Boston Spa.

The Rev. Job Johnson pictured in the latter years of his life.

Ruth E Storer – The Girl Preacher

In the introduction to my first two *Ye Olde Townships* books I raised the question of the mystery of a photograph of a young girl accompanied by the caption:

Ruth E Storer – The Girl Preacher – Denby.

What was so special about this picture, who was she and why was Ruth Storer important enough to have survived the decades bearing a family name not endemic to Denby, seemingly, a photograph out of nowhere.

I asked my readers for information about her but unfortunately none was forthcoming. My own enquiries have revealed further information.

Ruth Ellen Storer was born in 1896 in Barnby Don near Doncaster. She can be found in the 1901 census returns with her family:

John Storer	Head	34	Police Constable	Hucknall, Torkard, Notts.
Jessie Storer	Wife	30		Sheffield
Ruth Ellen Storer	Daughter	5		Barnby Don
Violet Jessie Storer	Daughter	4		Barnby Don
John Redvers Storer	Son	4m		Barnby Don

By the time 1911 census was recorded, PC John Storer had relocated to Upper Denby with his family.

John Storer	44	1867	Police Constable	Hucknall, Torkard, Notts.
Jessie Storer	40	1871		Sheffield
Violet Jessie Storer	14	1897	Power Loom Weaver	Barnby Don
John Redvers Storer	10	1901	Scholar	Barnby Don

So John Storer became the local policeman for Upper Denby and its environs. This explains the Upper Denby connection on the postcard but Ruth does not appear on the latter census return.

In fact she was a guest at the residence of Thomas and Mary Dales at Headingley, Leeds. Thomas Dales was a man of private means and employed three servants; he was a wealthy man. Ruth was noted to be fifteen years old, a visitor and an Evangelist.

Four years later she can be found in the Langham local news section of the Grantham Journal:

11 September 1915.
Visit of the Yorkshire Evangelist
On Sunday night last, Miss Ruth E Storer, the Yorkshire evangelist, preached two very excellent sermons in the Baptist Chapel, at which large congregations attended. She is well known as a

Ruth Storer, aged around 20 years old in 1911.

Ruth Storer with her mother, Jessie, circa 1901.

powerful and impressive speaker and has conducted services each evening up to Thursday. The final service is to be held on Monday. Special hymns were sung on these occasions.

No doubt encouraged by her parents, perhaps more significantly by her mother as she appears in various photographs with her daughter, why were 'girl preachers' so special?

The girl evangelist phenomenon became popular from around 1900, reaching its zenith in the 1920's. They were seen as a counter-type to the rapidly emerging 'flapper' and as an effective tool for revivalist Christianity.

The term 'flapper' was originally used to describe a very young prostitute though by the 1890's it largely meant a lively mid-teenage girl. The meaning then evolved to relate to young women who challenged the traditional role of women in society offering a considerable challenge to late Victorian values. They offered a culture war of old versus new. They wore short skirts, bobbed their hair, listened to jazz, wore make-up, smoked, drank alcohol, drove cars, treated sex in a casual manner and generally disdained anything that was considered, at that time, acceptable behaviour. They began working outside the home and advocated voting and women's rights.

The girl preachers or evangelists worked well as a contrast to the flappers for the press and public. Their devotion to plain living, hard work, religion and temperance stood in striking contrast to the racy flapper, who had come to define the modern girl. During the early decades of the twentieth century many young girls, some not even of school age, became 'girl preachers', perhaps something of a novelty, they proclaimed traditional values and spoke to large congregations. Their ages would endear them to an older generation but the carnage of World War One and the advent of the 'roaring twenties' signalled the end of an era for women and eventually the girl preachers were left behind by a society that had moved on.

What of Ruth after we last caught up with her in 1911?

On 26 December 1918 at Queen Street Chapel, Ossett she married a veteran of the First World War. Corporal Samuel Toon of 37 Intake Lane, Ossett aged 29, was the son of John Toon a grazier. Ruth was also living at 37 Intake Lane, aged 23; she was described as a Missioner. Ruth's younger sister and brother witnessed the marriage.

The final detail I have of her life is the ending of it. Ruth E Storer died in Lichfield, Staffordshire in 1961, aged 65.

At least now we know a little more about Ruth E Storer – The Girl Preacher, Denby.

Ruth Storer photographed sometime between 1911 and 1918.

Ruth Storer, the picture still notes that she was of Denby suggesting that it was taken prior to her marriage in 1918.

The George Inn – Upper Denby – Past and Present

The George Inn, Upper Denby has always been a subject close to my heart. Besides being my local, it has, over the years hosted a number of family events and indeed all ten of my book launches. I was pleased to be asked by the current owners to write a history of the Inn, a work still in progress as this book nears publication. This new research has thrown up some fascinating new details, which are included below.

The 'Olde' Inns of Denby

Name of Inn	Village	Earliest Date Noted	Last Date Noted
The Star	Upper Denby	1799	Closed 1904
The Wagon & Horses	Lower Denby	1799	Closed 1883
The Wellington	Upper Denby	1834 (the only historical mention)	
The New Inn	Upper Denby	1838	Closed 1963
The White Swan	High Flatts	1838	1883
The George Inn	Upper Denby	1852	Present
The Coach & Horses	Upper Denby	1865 (the only historical mention)	
The Dunkirk Inn	Lower Denby	1866	Present
The Sun Inn	Upper Denby	1883 (the only historical mention)	

NB1: The earliest year noted does not imply the foundation date for the Inn, just the first historical reference to it yet known. The Wagon & Horses and the Star dated well back into the eighteenth century and perhaps much earlier.

NB2: The three pubs at Upper Denby that have currently only one historical reference were almost certainly what were known as beer-houses, cheap, cheerful, small and unremarkable establishments. The Beer-house Act of 1830 enabled anyone to brew and sell beer on the premises on payment of 2 guineas for a licence. The intention was to wean the masses off drinking gin and increase competition between brewers which resulted in thousands of new beer-houses springing up countrywide. Some of these became dens for prostitutes and gambling and the haunts of criminals, though it is likely that the ones in Upper Denby were of a much tamer nature. It is also likely that all the Inns in the table above (excluding the oldest two) began life as beer-houses (including the George). A change in the law took place in 1869 placing ale-houses back under the jurisdiction of the Local Justices which saw the gradual closure of many of the beer-houses and saw the survivors become fully licensed public houses.

Before we examine the early history of the George Inn we can learn a little of some of the occurrences at the other nearby establishments from local newspapers:

Bradford Observer 16 July 1846
Death By Drowning – Another Warning to Bathers

An inquest was held on Tuesday, before Mr G D Barker, the deputy coroner, at the house of Mr John Firth, the Star Inn, Upper Denby, on the body of Levi Hanson, a 'navvy', who was unfortunately drowned whilst bathing in Rumfit Mill Dam, on Sunday morning last. Robert Rice of Upper Denby, labourer deposed: The deceased worked on the Sheffield and

Huddersfield railway near Denby. On Sunday morning last, between ten and eleven o'clock, I and the deceased went to bathe together in Rumfit Mill Dam; we both stripped, neither of us could swim and I went into the water to try the depth, I got our of my depth but eventually recovered by footing. The deceased, who had bathed there before, jumped in lower down; he got out of his depth, he cried out, and I saw him sinking. I then tried to get to him but found that the water was too deep; he came twice to the surface, and then sunk to rise no more. The body was not got out of the water until three o'clock in the afternoon and life was quite extinct. Joseph Hanson, Uncle to the deceased, corroborated the evidence. Verdict, 'accidentally drowned'. Deceased was 24 years of age and has left a wife and six children.

(NB: Rumfit Mill Dam should read Gumfit Mill Dam, i.e. Gunthwaite).

Sheffield Telegraph 9 February 1865.
Turning a Landlord out of his own house

J Wormald, landlord of the Coach & Horses Inn, Upper Denby, was charged with assaulting his wife on the 2nd inst. From the statement of the wife it appeared that after a years marriage they did not agree, and she told her lord and master that he had better return to his mother. The attraction at the Coach and Horses not being very extensive, nothing loth, he took his ladies advice and went to his maternal parent, where he stopped for about ten weeks. He, however, returned on Thursday night last and believing that he was lord of the castle, went upstairs and, having divested himself of his boots and coat, was all but ready to get into bed, when Mrs Wormald put in an appearance, ordering him out of the house and, on his non-compliance, 'pitched into him'. Finding she was getting the worst of the battle, she called out for assistance, which was promptly rendered by a stalwart youth named Burgess, who rolled the landlord downstairs, shoved him out of the Coach & Horses and sent his boots and coat after him. The bench dismissed the case and it is not likely that Mr Burgess will come to grief for forcibly ejecting a man from his own house.

Leeds Times 29 September 1883

Joshua Carter at the White Swan, High Flatts requested a spirit licence.
Charles Kilner of the Prospect Hotel, Denby Dale, asked that the full licence of the Wagon & Horses Inn, Dunkirk, be transferred to his house.

Sheffield Independent 10 January 1883
Singular Fatality at Denby

Yesterday an inquest was held at the Sun Inn, Upper Denby, near Barnsley, touching the death of Mary Peace, widow of Upper Denby aged 66 years who died suddenly on Saturday. Deceased, who had been washing, was laughing and talking by the fireside on Saturday night in her usual health, when she suddenly threw her head back and died almost immediately. Deceased had not complained of being unwell. A verdict to the effect that deceased died from natural causes was returned.

Here we can see the evidence of a further two 'pubs' in Upper Denby, taking the current total up to six. Returning to the George Inn:

The Denby Enclosure Award Map dated 1802 shows that the buildings and land that were later to become the George Inn were originally owned by William Bosville, a member of the family that had been the Lords of nearby Gunthwaite since the fourteenth century. The original building on the site (the bottom floor of which is now the lounge room) is of at least eighteenth century origin and was originally a farm, probably associated with the buildings across the road, which were also farm buildings, though these have long been converted into cottages. Before its history as a pub the building was used as a sanatorium, perhaps upon similar lines to the one at High Flatts, as a refuge for inebriate women.

The George and the land around it was later acquired by the Norton's group up until 1877 when it was bought from their trustees. Local newspapers advertised it as a:

> *Freehold Public House, known as the George Inn at Upper Denby with stable, carriage house, cow-house, cottage and large garden, currently occupied by Mrs Taylor (Nancy).*

In 1882 it was noted by the Barnsley Permanent Building Society that the pub was owned by Reuben and James Senior and that it was occupied by George Taylor. The origins of the George owe much to a local colliery owner and brewer. Seth Senior and Sons brewery began trading in 1829, the story goes that Seth borrowed a sovereign to begin brewing in his own cottage and became so successful he was able to start the business, where he was joined by his sons, Reuben and James. They established and took over many pubs around their Shepley area, including the 'Sovereign' named as a reminder of their humble beginnings. They became responsible for both the George and New Inn at Denby and although not in existence at the pub's origins they were also to take over the Star. On 21st November 1946 Senior's were taken over by Hammond's brewery of Lockwood which signalled the demise of their name in pub ownership.

The Taylor family, the first Landlord's of the George Inn

The first mention of the George Inn occurs in 1852 when we can find Enoch Taylor as the landlord. Enoch was born in Upper Denby in 1820, the fourth son of George Taylor and Rachel Haigh. In the Denby baptism records of 1850 he was noted to be a coal-miner and in the census returns of 1851 he was recorded as working as a fancy weaver. By the time of the birth of his daughter Ann, in 1852, Enoch is described as a beer-house keeper. Keeping an alehouse as a second occupation was the norm and we can find Enoch working as a colliery manager for Seth Senior at Kirkburton in 1864. As the Senior family were the leaseholders of the George it is likely that his association with the family of brewers goes back to the time he was noted to be working as a miner in 1850. His tenure at the George also meant that he could use the term farmer as an occupation. So, coal-miner, fancy weaver, farmer and innkeeper were all recorded as his professions.

Enoch, known as Nack, was a fascinating character and features in a large number of newspaper reports during the nineteenth century, a number of which I have published in previous volumes. He married Rebecca Booth and had at least five children before Rebecca's death in 1866 aged 40.

During his time at the George he was imprisoned in York Castle Gaol as an insolvent debtor due to acts of vandalism and trespass when he tried to open up a new doorway into the pub. Evidently Enoch was of strong and wilful character, as the following two newspaper reports will show, but this time he was imprisoned for his stubbornness and the fact that he was totally unable to afford to pay the fine and damages imposed upon him – hence he went to debtors prison.

Yorkshire Gazette 26 March 1859 - Malicious Trespass

Enoch Taylor of Upper Denby, coal-miner. In 1855 and up to the beginning of last year, the insolvent was a beer housekeeper at Upper Denby. He had no entrance to the back part of his premises and he consequently pulled down a portion of a wall and made a doorway. To enter the house in this way a trespass was committed to the land immediately adjoining it. The insolvent was discharged from pulling down the wall but he persisted in so doing. The wall was rebuilt two or three times but it was demolished again by the insolvent. A writ was served upon him and the damaged and the costs of the action amounted to upwards of £40. His honour remanded the insolvent to be remanded for three months from the date of the vesting order.

York Herald 26 March 1859 - Trespass at Upper Denby

….it appeared there was only one entrance. After he had entered upon its occupation he made another entrance at the back of the premises and so committed the trespass. From the evidence of Mr Dransfield, solicitor, Penistone, it seemed in the Spring of last year, the insolvent having shortly before left the beerhouse, an inquiry took place before the Under Sheriff of York with respect to the trespass and that damaged were assessed at £5 7s 6d, the costs amounting upwards of £85. The property upon which the trespass was committed belongs to a gentleman named Bosville whose fence wall had been pulled down as was alleged by the defendant two or three times after it had been re-built. A doorway had also been made in his premises, the soil taken from the land and a regular pathway made. The insolvent denied pulling down the wall, but His Honour had no doubt on the subject and therefore remanded the insolvent for three months from the date of the vesting order viz. 28 January 1859.

At this time in England, debtors owing money could be easily detained by the courts for indefinite periods, being kept in debtor's prisons. Acts of parliament in 1831 and 1861 had begun the process of reform in this area, but further reform was felt necessary. Prisons were overflowing with debtors, a situation the government could not continue and a further Act in 1869 significantly reduced the ability of the courts to detain those in debt, although some provisions were retained.

After he completed his sentence, Enoch returned to the George, which had continued to be run in his absence by his wife, Rebecca. He continued to appear regularly in the local newspapers, sometimes as an accomplished marksman other times in more unseemly incidents as we can see, from the following recently discovered newspaper reports:

Sheffield Independent 5 September 1857

Enoch Taylor, the George Inn applied through Mr Tyas. The application was for the transfer of the licence from the White Swan to his house. The application was signed by Messrs. Norton and the principal ratepayers in the neighbourhood.

Sheffield Independent 10 August 1861 - The Publicans and the Census

Enoch Taylor, beer-house keeper, Upper Denby was charged with having his house open after the hour of ten at night on the 28th ult. The offence was acknowledged on the grounds that the population of Denby parish exceeded 2500 inhabitants. Enoch Taylor fined 1s and costs. He was told that any re-offence would incur the full penalty as the census had not yet been officially declared.

Huddersfield Chronicle 24 December 1864 - Robbery at Coal Pit

Walter Jackson was charged with stealing two pairs of overalls, the property of Enoch Taylor, an innkeeper at Denby and Manager at Mr Seth Senior's colliery at Kirkburton. The evidence against the prisoner being conclusive he was sentenced to two months imprisonment.

Huddersfield District Chronicle 21 July 1866 - Denby – Accident

On Tuesday an accident occurred near this place to a party returning from Penistone Station. It seems Mr Enoch Taylor, farmer and innkeeper of Denby, with his brother, son and other members of the family had been to Penistone Station for a box and were returning home in a spring cart about 8:30. Mr Taylor having charge of the reigns. When about turning an abrupt corner of the road from Ingbirchworth into Denby, one of the parties remarked to Mr Taylor 'mind and keep off the corner'. The party who gave the caution seized the reigns and unfortunately pulled the wrong one when the horse ran violently against the wall at the corner, overturned the vehicle and pitched the seven occupants into the road. Beyond a black eye and a severe shaking, none of the party were injured. The trap was broken to some extent but not so much as to prevent the party from proceeding home by it.

Huddersfield Chronicle 20 April 1867 - Denby – Pigeon Shooting

On Monday night a pigeon shooting match came off in Mr Charles Wood's field, Upper Denby, between Enoch Taylor and Aaron Hanwell, both innkeepers of that village. The stakes were £10 a side each man having fifteen birds. Taylor proved the victor by killing 7 birds to his opponents 6.

Sheffield Independent 12 December 1867 - Local Sporting – Pigeon Shooting Match at Upper Denby

On Thursday at Denby near Penistone a shooting match for £5 a side took place at the house of Mr Enoch Taylor, the George Inn, Denby. The shooters were Enoch, alias 'Nach' Taylor and Joseph, alias 'Tip' Whitaker. Taylor was the favourite at slight odds. The conditions were 1oz of shot, 21 yards rise and 60 boundary, each man to shoot at nine birds. The match proved a one-sided affair as will be seen by the score: Taylor 5 out of 8, Whitaker 2 out of 7.

Sheffield Independent 23 December 1869 - Denby – A Number of Assaults

Yesterday at Barnsley Court House, the sitting Magistrates were occupied for several hours in hearing a number of serious assault cases which took place at Denby on 4 November. The first case taken was that against William Taylor who was charged with assaulting George Beaumont and stabbing him with a pocketknife. The prosecution stated that he was standing at the door of a stable on the day named with a person named Fretwell. Whilst he was talking to the latter, Oliver Taylor, Enoch Taylor, William Taylor and a man named Sharp went through the yard along a footpath. Enoch Taylor got hold of another mans arm, who was present and said 'don't talk to Pickford's thief'. Some stones were then thrown and William Taylor pulled out his knife and, addressing the prosecutor said 'I will give thee this' and he at once stabbed him in the back of the thigh. Several witnesses were called amongst whom was James Edward Beanland, assistant to Mr Dowse, surgeon of Skelmanthorpe who said he was called in to see the prosecutor on the 4th ult. He found him suffering from a puncture wound in the back part of the thigh which 2½ inches in depth and about an inch in length. The wound was such as might have been inflicted with a pocketknife. His trousers were cut through and he was confined to bed for several days. The bench, before deciding the case went on to hear another arising out of the same affray. Oliver Taylor, William Taylor, Enoch Taylor and David Tyas were charged with assaulting William Fretwell at the same time and place. There were also five other summonses returned for assaults which were not heard. Each of the defendants in the assault cases was fined 5s + costs and committed the defendant William Taylor for trial to the ensuing sessions on the charge of cutting and wounding.

After the death of his first wife, Rebecca, in 1866, Enoch entered into his second marriage with Nancy Dawson, also from Upper Denby. The marriage was not a long one, as Enoch was not destined for a long life. Still involved with coal-mining, and in particular, surveying his time ran out in 1870 in the most tragic circumstances possible:

Morpeth Herald 30 July 1870 - Shocking Explosion in a Colliery near Barnsley

A serious explosion of gas took place on Friday afternoon in a colliery at Low Mill near Cawthorne belonging to J S Stanhope Esq. of Canon Hall. It appears that three gentlemen named Henry Ellis of Denby, colliery owner, Mr H Wood, landlord of the Sovereign Inn near Shepley and Mr Enoch Taylor, landlord of the George Inn, Denby, were in treaty for working the colliery which for a time has been laid idle. The workings were approached by a day hole and at about 2pm in the afternoon they went into the mine with a candle to examine the workings. Whilst they were in the pit a terrific explosion of gas took place, which seriously injured them. Mr Taylor, who was nearest the gas when it exploded was shockingly burnt about the face, hands, neck and head.

All the men involved died of their injuries, Enoch was just fifty years old.

The pub continued to be run by his wife, Nancy, almost certainly aided by her sons and by her brother in law, George Taylor, whom she eventually married, at which event he took over as the landlord of the George. Shortly after Enoch's death Nancy found herself in trouble for trying to sell some surveying instruments that Enoch had borrowed prior to his death:

Huddersfield Chronicle 13 July 1872 - Holmfirth County Court
An Action to Recover Mining Instruments

Mr Thomas Haigh, coal merchant of Denby Dale sought to recover several instruments used in mining operations from Nancy Taylor. Mr Haigh, amongst several other things was a coal merchant and the late Mr Enoch Taylor was engaged by the plaintiff in mining operations. Mr Haigh had some very valuable mining instruments which he lent from time to time to the late Mr Enoch Taylor. About three years ago Mr Taylor went to borrow these articles again and they had not since been returned to the plaintiff. At the time of Mr Taylor's death, which took place in 1870, they had been demanded from him and after his death they were demanded from his widow, who however, denied all knowledge of having had them. One of the articles, the 'latching glass' valued at 11 guineas had been taken by Mrs Taylor, after her husbands death to Mr Wemyss of Canon Hall. She wanted to sell it to that gentleman, but he, suspecting that something was wrong, returned it to her, informing Mr Haigh of the transaction by letter, which was sent to him by the same courier. Strange to say, however, that the letter was intercepted by Mrs Taylor, which would almost show that she was aware that the goods belonged to Mr Haigh. A sale took place at Mr Taylor's death but the articles in question were not then sold. The plaintiff now sought an order for the return of the instruments. Mr Thomas Haigh, coal merchant then deposed that the late Mr Enoch Taylor used to be in his employ. Witness lent him a latching glass; two boxes of instruments, a parallel ruler and a land measure chain. Witness lent them to him himself, to survey some pits, as he said. The last time that the witness had them in his possession was about three years ago when he went to survey for Mr Richard Firth and Mr Henry Hellawell. Witness sent his son to ask for them back and he sent his son to ask his widow for them back after the death of Mr Enoch Taylor. Witness also instructed Mr Booth to write for the goods but no answer had been received from Mrs Taylor. Cross-examined by Mr Armitage. It was not a fact that the late Mr Taylor had had the goods in his possession for fourteen or fifteen years, nor had witness ever made a present to him of them in consideration of services the late Mr Taylor had rendered to his (witnesses) son. He never rendered any services to witness's son. Witness would swear that he had the articles in his possession during the last fourteen or fifteen years. When he left witnesses service the goods were on the plaintiff's premises. When he entered the service of Mr Seth Senior, Mr Taylor asked witness if he would lend him the instruments again and witness complied with his request. He brought them back in 1866. Witness did not think he had had them from 1860 to 1866. Mr Taylor had never had them in his possession for three years uninterruptedly. He had not sold any portion of the goods during his lifetime. Mr Wemyss, who was then called for the plaintiff said he had lost a latching glass. He got a glass from Mrs Taylor in its place, but it was soon afterwards identified by Mr Haigh who claimed it as his property. Mr Swift, mining engineer identified the glass as Mr Haigh's property. The glass was not in working order but witness would have given £7 or £8 for it as it was. Mr Wemyss sent it back to Mrs Taylor with a note by the same courier for Mr Haigh, telling him what he had done. Witness had the glass in his possession from the latter part of August 1870 to the beginning of the present year. George Norton, carrier, proved taking a box for Mr Wemyss to Mrs Taylor. He also received a letter from Mr Wemyss for Mr Haigh but Mrs Taylor took it from him and promised to forward it to Mr Haigh. Mr Richard Firth deposed that he knew the late Mr Taylor and that he had heard him say that the glass in question was the property of Mr Haigh. Walter Haigh, son of the plaintiff was then called. He stated that by order of his father, he went to the late Mr Taylor and asked him for the latching glass. He then said he had a little bit of latching to do and wanted to send it back soon after. That was in June 1870, shortly before his death. In August witness went to Mrs Taylor and asked for the goods but she said she had not got them. Mr Armitage contended for the defence that there had been no case made out for anything else than the latching glass. He said Mrs Taylor had been left a widow by an unfortunate accident which killed her husband in very bad circumstances. Oliver Taylor, a delver of Denby was then called. He stated that the plaintiff told him that he had made a present of the latching glass to Mr Enoch Taylor for his services to him and his son. That was about fifteen years ago. His honour stated that in the case of Mr Taylor and Mr Haigh there had evidently been a kindly feeling running between employer and employed. Verdict for the plaintiff for the latching glass. £7 10s, not to be enforced if the glass was returned. The glass was formally given up in court.

NB: A latching glass was used to make an underground survey with a dial and chain in order to mark out on the surface the position of the workings underneath.

Life at the George continued with its usual array of incidents, the following is but an example:

Huddersfield Chronicle 22 November 1873 - Theft of a Horse and Cart
William Wilson, confectioner, Back-Buxton Road, was charged with having stolen, on the 12th November, a horse and cart, of the value of £40, the property of Joseph Wood, confectioner, Union Street. The complainant said: I am a confectioner, and on the 12th of November last I took my horse and cart, with a quantity of confectionery and went hawking. As I was returning home, and had got to Taylor Hill, I met the prisoner and we both went to the Town Hall Inn at Lockwood, where we had two glasses of ale each. I left my horse and cart at the door. Before we had finished the second glass, the prisoner went out, and I afterwards found my horse and cart had been taken away. Not being able to find them I gave information to the police. On Sunday, the 16th inst., I went with Police Constable Parker to the George Inn, Denby and there found my horse and cart. There was

an overcoat, 118lbs of spice, 52 rolls of tape and a quantity of worsted balls and smallwares missing, these I value at £5. William Tyas, shopkeeper, Upper Denby, said: On Thursday night, the 13th inst. The prisoner called at my house. I was feeding the pigs at the time. I afterwards went to the George Inn and saw the prisoner there. We went together to my shop. He had a horse and cart with him. He showed me a quantity of spice in bottles and spice in cans. He offered them to me for sale. I bought five pounds of humbugs and cough drops. I paid him 2s and he gave me the tin canister to put them in. The spices produced, which I handed to Police Constable Parker, are part of those I bought. Ann Taylor, the next witness, said: The prisoner called at the George Inn, Denby on the night in question and asked me if he could stay all night. I told him that we could not accommodate him that night and he then asked if he could leave the horse and cart and that he would come again on the Friday morning for them. I told him that he could leave them. He left them and the horse and cart stayed at our house until they were fetched by the Police. George Micklethwaite, grocer, Upper Denby said: The prisoner called at my house on Thursday night, the 13th instant. He asked me to buy some cough drops and I bought nine pounds of them. I bought three bottles of other spice. I paid him 6s or 6s 6d. The spice now produced, which I handed to Police-constable Parker are part of what I bought. Police-constable John Beaumont said: I apprehended the prisoner on Thursday night, the 13th inst., and charged him with stealing a horse and cart and a quantity of spice. He replied 'I know nothing at all about it. I have never seen it, neither the horse nor the cart'. I found the prosecutor's coat at the lodgings of the prisoner. The horse and cart were found through the Chief constable advertising. The prisoner was drunk when I apprehended him. Police-constable Parker said: On the 16th instant I went to Upper Denby and found the horse and cart belonging to the prosecutor. There was a quantity of spice in it. I received five pounds of spice from William Tyas, nine and half pounds of cough drops and six pounds of lemon drops from George Micklethwaite and a dozen of worsted balls, two cards of metal buttons, a card of linen buttons and a dozen of braid from Mrs Silverwood. In reply to the Bench, the prisoner said he was guilty, but he was drunk at the time. He was fully committed for trial.

George Taylor remained as the landlord until at least 1889, but by 1891, Enoch and Rebecca's son, Alfred had taken over. Alfred, though very likely to have been involved with helping out in the pub, had worked as a general labourer up until 1886 when his occupation changes to that of steelworker. He married Ann Wing, a relative of Sam Wing who became the landlord of the New Inn prior to the outbreak of World War One. Their time at the George ended between 1904 and 1909, meaning that the Taylor family had an association of over fifty years with the pub, far longer than anyone who came after them.

The Taylor Family

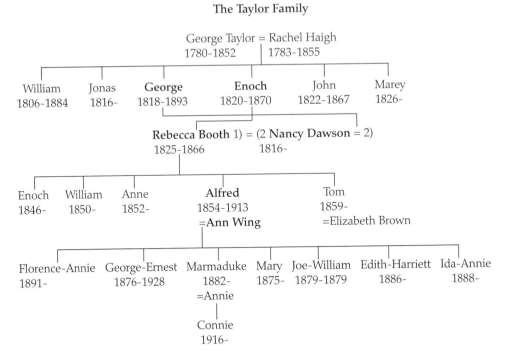

(NB: Names in bold type were Landlord's/Landlady's of the George. All the latter were born and lived in Upper Denby).

The Present Day Inn

In 2008 the pub entered a new era. As with all such establishments the pub has had it fair share of good and bad times over the years but as is well known the traditional British pub is in serious decline. Since the year 2000 and up until 2010, 8,800 public houses have closed, never to re-open. The current rate of closure is estimated to be 26 per week averaging around 1,300 a year. In 2008 the George was left unoccupied until the Wyatt family, from Ingbirchworth took over the tenancy. The pub increased its popularity during their tenure but the recession and the restrictions involved whilst working with the brewery that owned the pub, Admiral Taverns, proved frustrating and limited any progression of the business. Ever enterprising, the Wyatt family successfully negotiated with Admiral Taverns and announced, by way of a village circular, dated Monday 19 November 2012, that they had completed the sale of the pub 'lock, stock and barrels'. Since that time, the pub has begun to look forward with more confidence, holding regular live music nights, a weekly quiz, country walks, serving home made pies and hosting other special events. Its Casque Mark Accredited quality ales have recently led the pub to achieve possibly its highest award yet when it was named the Camra Huddersfield Branch Autumn Pub of the Season for 2013. Camra gives this award for not only the high quality of the cask

The owners and staff of the George Inn, Upper Denby in December 2013. Back row, left to right: Tony Wyatt, Douglas Wyatt, Dean Wyatt, Shane Wyatt. Front row, left to right: Emily Woodhead, Ellie Lodge, Lucy Price, Zoe Wyatt, Celia Wyatt.

ale served but also overall cleanliness, atmosphere and commitment to the community served by the pub. Paul Laxton, Chairman of the Huddersfield and District branch of Camra made the presentation in December 2013 to joint Landlords, Dean and Tony Wyatt and family after a night of Carol singing with Shepley Band.

The next major venture for the Wyatt family and the George Inn was the hosting of a Steam Rally on the weekend of 17 and 18 May 2014, in order to raise money for the Yorkshire Air Ambulance. It proved to be an event, which galvanised and brought the local community together. The Ward family of Upper Denby were to prove instrumental in the event being possible at all by using their connections within the world of steam in order to attract a serious number of exhibits for the weekend. John, Andrew, Brendan, Darren and Tom Ward, three generations working together, had, over the years assembled an impressive collection of steam vehicles of their own and were fundamental to the success of the event. The Wyatt family ably assisted by

The award certificate, given by the Huddersfield branch of Camra to the George Inn, Autumn Pub of the Year 2013.

The fleet of engines owned by the Ward family of Upper Denby at the front of the George.

Alison Brook and her family of Upper Denby gradually created and prepared an array of attractions and undertook all aspects of publicity. A small army of volunteers was recruited to aid in the rolls of stewarding, safety, selling raffle tickets and collecting money for the Air Ambulance. All that was required was good weather.

Blessed with two days of warm sunshine the weekend began with live music from Dominic & Kieran on the Friday night. Almost twenty steam engines, wagons, rollers and miniatures were in position by 10am on Saturday morning. Large crowds were entertained over the two days by: Shepley Band, Winston's Pennine Jazz, arts and crafts provided by Artisan Fayre (of Penistone), the Barnsley Longswords and the Rhubarb Tarts Morris Dancers. A flypast was arranged for both days along with a road run on the Saturday, undertaken by the steam vehicles in convoy from the George to the Fountain Inn at Ingbirchworth. Food was available including a barbecue, the Yummy Yorkshire Ice Cream Company, and the Big Yellow Chippy Bus (which sold out). Further live music was provided on the Saturday night by the Following, a covers band, appropriately based in Upper Denby. To mark the occasion the pub had organised a specially brewed ale for the day, named 'Full Steam'. Eight firkins (in nine gallon barrels) equalling 576 pints had sold out by Saturday evening, raising a further 50pence per pint for the charity. Commemorative glass tankards and tulip glasses were also produced, the tankard selling out within hours. Thousands of raffle tickets were also sold, again for the charity, leading to 120 winners. In order to involve the entire village a best decorated house competition was also held, harking back to the Silver Jubilee celebrations of King George V. The theme was simply

A warm, sunny day creates a chocolate box scene at the front of the George, courtesy of the Ward family vehicles.

Steam engines and wagon in the car park.

Great Britain and a large number of enterprising householders took up the challenge. Upper Denby was festooned in red, white and blue bunting and flags with some marking the hundredth anniversary of the First World War. The £100 prize for the best in the village went to Stuart and Yvonne Townend on Green Acre Drive. The village church and school were both open all weekend displaying history and serving refreshments. To complete the weekend and with a nod to a great Denby Dale tradition, two giant pies were cooked and turned into 275 portions which sold out within half an hour. The total amount raised for the Air Ambulance was an amazing £6462.46.

The steam rally was a meeting of old and new, an appropriate way to end this book. A village embracing a once familiar bygone age at an event where the very young and the older generations mixed and mingled, played, laughed and reminisced and let the past hold their attention for a short while. The past, our history, made us what we are now, personally and collectively and it is an amazing and true fact that it can and does unite generations and communities in the twenty-first century.

Chronological Table of the Landlords of the George Inn

NB: It should be noted that some of the early dates given are not terms of tenancy but the years known in which the pub was occupied by that person.

1852-1870	Enoch Taylor
1871/1881	Nancy Taylor
1882/1889	George Taylor
1891/1904	Alfred Taylor
1909	Joseph Airton
1917	Benjamin Slater
1926	Edward 'Teddy' Daniels
1927	George Henry 'Genny' Buckley
1930-1958	Frank & Mabel Widdowson
1958-1970	Jim & Dot Barber
1970-1992	Roy Barraclough
1992-1993	Martin & Carol Brook
1993-1999	Steven & Jill Slater
1999-2000	Ken Hunt
2000-2002	Joan Eastwood & Clare Davis (Clare solely in 2002)
2002-2004	Graeme & Tracy Mallinson (Graeme solely between 2005-2007)
2007-2008	Dennis Tyson & Sharon Lofthouse
2008 - Present	Dean & Tony Wyatt

Pump clip, advertising the ale specially
brewed for the event.

Steam engines in the pub car park.

Steam engines and roller on display in the car park at the George.

Beautifully restored relics of a bygone age take over the pub car park for a weekend.

The crowds begin to gather on the Saturday afternoon in the pub car park.

The Barnsley Longswords entertain the crowds.

Young and old alike are entertained amidst the steam from the engines.

Andrew Ward (in one of the family vehicles) and Alan Clegg (both of Upper Denby) depart on the road run from the George, no doubt in search of refreshment at the Fountain Inn at Ingbirchworth.

The Turner Brothers engine sets out on the road run.

The steamroller, of L B Donn and son passing St. Johns Church and heading onto Falledge Lane.

A steam engine on the return route from Ingbirchworth passes Milnes Row, about to turn into the George car park.

The steam engine belonging to Roy Lee, illuminated at the front of the George.

Tony and Celia Wyatt, serving some of the 275 portions of pie on the Sunday.